Jumpstart RTI

USING RTI IN YOUR ELEMENTARY SCHOOL RIGHT NOW

SUSAN L. HALL

CORWIN
A SAGE Company

FOR INFORMATION:

Corwin
A SAGE Company
2455 Teller Road
Thousand Oaks, California 91320
(800) 233-9936
Fax: (800) 417-2466
www.corwin.com

SAGE Ltd.
1 Oliver's Yard
55 City Road
London EC1Y 1SP
United Kingdom

SAGE India Pvt. Ltd.
B 1/I 1 Mohan Cooperative
Industrial Area
Mathura Road, New Delhi 110 044
India

SAGE Asia-Pacific Pte. Ltd.
33 Pekin Street #02-01
Far East Square
Singapore 048763

Acquisitions Editor: Arnis Burvikovs
Associate Editor: Desirée Bartlett
Editorial Assistant: Kimberly Greenberg
Permissions Editor: Karen Ehrmann
Production Editor: Jane Haenel
Typesetter: C&M Digitals (P) Ltd.
Proofreader: Gretchen Treadwell
Indexer: Maria Sosnowski
Cover Designer: Michael Dubowe

Printed in the United States of America

Library of Congress Cataloging-in-Publication Data

Hall, Susan L. (Susan Long)

Jumpstart RTI : using RTI in your elementary school right now / Susan L. Hall.

p. cm.
Includes bibliographical references and index.

ISBN 978-1-4129-8172-9 (pbk.)

1. Reading (Elementary)—United States.
2. Learning disabled children—Education—United States.
3. Reading—Remedial teaching—United States.
4. Response to intervention (Learning disabled children)
I. Title.

LB1573.H1717 2011 372.43—dc22 2010044640

This book is printed on acid-free paper.

11 12 13 14 15 10 9 8 7 6 5 4 3 2 1

Contents

Additional materials and resources related to *Jumpstart RTI: Using RTI in Your Elementary School Right Now* can be found at http://my.95percentgroup.com/Jumpstart.

Publisher's Acknowledgments

Corwin would like to thank the following individuals for their editorial insight:

Alice Hom, Principal
Yung Wing Elementary PS 124
New York City, New York

Barbara P. Misuraca, NBCT
Exceptional Needs Specialist
Detroit Public Schools
Detroit, Michigan

Kathy Tritz-Rhodes, Principal
Marcus-Meriden-Cleghorn Schools
Marcus and Cleghorn, Iowa

About the Author

Susan L. Hall, EdD, is a consultant specializing in teacher training and early reading. She is founder and president of an educational consulting and professional development company called 95 Percent Group, Inc. The company provides consulting and teacher training to districts and schools in response to intervention (RTI) in early reading. 95 Percent Group specializes in how to use early literacy screening data to place students in groups for tiers of intervention, as well as instructional strategies to address specific skill deficits. Susan is a nationally certified trainer of *DIBELS* and *LETRS.* She is author of *I've DIBEL'd, Now What?* and *Implementing Response to Intervention: A Principal's Guide.* She is coauthor with Louisa Moats of two books, *Straight Talk About Reading* and *Parenting a Struggling Reader,* as well as *LETRS Module 7: Teaching Phonics, Word Study, and the Alphabetic Principle,* Second Edition. Susan can be reached at shall@95percentgroup.com.

Introduction

The purpose of *Jumpstart RTI* is to assist teachers, principals, and district staff in efficiently and effectively implementing response-to-intervention practices to improve an elementary school's reading scores.

WHY THIS BOOK IS NEEDED

Much has been written about response to intervention, or RTI. Educators don't need another "me too" book; *Jumpstart RTI* is different. The motivation to write this book came from watching many schools waste a great deal of time trying to figure out how to implement RTI. The books currently available on this subject include the following topics:

- Definition of RTI
- Overview of RTI
- The history of how the ratification of IDEA 2004 led to RTI
- A three-tier pyramid showing that smaller numbers of students need Tier II and even smaller numbers need Tier III
- The legal foundation for RTI as a means to identify students for special education services
- Forms for self-assessment before launching RTI
- Forms for identifying RTI team members
- Forms for reporting data
- Forms for many other things

Author's note: Throughout the book, the pronoun *her* is often used when referring to a teacher. Using this pronoun avoids the awkward language of "his or her," and its predominance reflects the high proportion of female teachers in elementary schools. The author does not intend to exclude male teachers and asks for the reader's understanding in this decision. When referring to an individual student, the pronouns *he* and *his* are often used to differentiate a student from a teacher. Additionally, when the author uses the words *we* or *our*, she is referring to herself and her consulting company, 95 Percent Group, Inc.

Jumpstart RTI is practical, results oriented, and evidence based, focusing on practical tips on how to initiate RTI in a school. I've been in a fortunate position of watching hundreds of schools during the past 10 years while assisting them in implementing early literacy intervention practices, now named RTI. The suggestions in this book originate from my observations of schools implementing RTI and determining what it takes for a smooth implementation. This book is a bit shorter on forms than most other books on this topic. It also does not position RTI as driven by a legal or regulatory approach to the qualification procedure for special education services. Although that's important, RTI is so much more than special education qualification; it offers schools a unique opportunity to nurture a paradigm shift that affects how reading skills are measured, how struggling readers are identified and addressed, and how teachers think about meeting the needs of *all* students.

This book is results oriented because my perspective is consistently riveted to achieving gains in student reading scores. Not only is data used to make every key decision about the appropriate instruction for an individual student, but it's also paramount to determine whether RTI is making a difference for the student population as a whole. Improvement in student reading is what really matters. Just like a race-car driver's job is not done until she safely crosses the finish line, hopefully in first place, an educator's job is not done until a school's RTI practices result in at least 95% of students reading at benchmark levels.

The suggestions and recommendations in this book are all evidence based. During the past 10 years, I've been carefully tracking the student data in schools that are implementing these practices. Although I've recommended some practices in the 2005 publication of the book *I've DIBEL'd, Now What?* most of the information in this book has emerged since then. My consulting company has amassed a great deal of data about best practices by tracking curriculum-based measure (CBM) and screener data on thousands of students taught by the hundreds of teachers we serve via professional development during multiyear client engagements. We can see which practices bring the greatest gains in student achievement.

The evidence is clear that if schools follow the recommendations in this book, student reading scores will rise to high levels. Equally clear is how very difficult it is for schools to implement some of these practices, not because they are challenging but because they require a high level of staff buy-in and strong leadership from administrators. When either staff commitment or leadership is missing, the implementation suffers and gains in student reading scores are not as strong as they could be.

OVERVIEW OF THE CONTENTS

Having stated that a focus on gains in reading scores is paramount, it will be no surprise that the first chapter starts with the end in mind. It's a story about one district that effectively implements response to intervention, the gains in their students' reading scores, and the path the district took to get there.

Chapter 1. Ninety-Five Percent of Students at Benchmark Is Achievable: A District Example: How high should you expect your school's reading scores to be if you implement the recommendations in this book? Schools need to set ambitious goals. Many researchers are shocked at the results that our client schools achieve. We aren't shocked anymore; we are motivated. So how will you know how high to set goals? Chapter 1 addresses this question from the perspective of a single school and also from that of a medium-sized district. It's much easier to point out an example of a single teacher or school whose results are fabulous. It's far different to see how an entire district implemented RTI and, after five years, how 95% of students reached benchmark across 38 schools at multiple grade levels.

Chapter 2. Getting Ready: Many books and RTI speakers recommend an extensive planning process before launching RTI. This book takes a different approach. While planning is imperative, Chapter 2 describes the planning that is critical to articulate a "call to action" and to build staff buy-in and commitment. Also included are tips on how to address resistance or reluctance from teachers who would rather continue to do the same thing they have been doing than embrace the changes needed. Most schools designate an RTI coordinator; the responsibilities of this role are outlined.

Chapter 3. Getting Started: This chapter describes several structural components that affect the number of minutes of intervention instruction and addresses allocating time for intervention groups, determining who will teach groups, and choosing a delivery model. Best results are achieved when the school's master schedule includes intervention blocks. Determining who teaches the intervention groups and the content of instruction during group time is imperative.

Chapter 4. Analyzing Data and Forming Groups: One of the main messages of this chapter is that CBMs do an excellent job at identifying which students are at risk of later reading difficulties but don't provide information that enables teachers to pinpoint skill deficits. The CBM data provide adequate information to determine the next steps, that is, to decide whether to administer a diagnostic screener and, if so, which screener is appropriate. Schools making the most progress are placing students in skill groups based on diagnostic screener data in addition to CBM data. Which assessment to use for progress monitoring is addressed, along with some guidance on how grade-level teams can form initial groups and regroup after collecting progress-monitoring data.

Chapter 5. Delivering Effective Intervention Instruction: What does effective intervention instruction look like? Chapter 5 begins with a description of the characteristics that make intervention different from whole-class or other small-group instruction. Activities should follow explicit and systematic instruction and serve as practice for students after the skill has been taught. There are many misconceptions about materials and programs; many schools are confused about what *research based* means. They believe that they need to purchase programs that are stamped *research based* and then attempt to implement them with fidelity. In this chapter, I'll explain the issues related to this belief and recommend that schools should be using materials that include research-based strategies and invest in professional development to help teachers learn to make good decisions during instruction.

Chapter 6. Initiating a Problem-Solving Process: Nearly every document written about RTI mentions the need for facilitating problem-solving meetings. Chapter 6 includes a sample agenda for a 15- to 20-minute team meeting to decide whether to intensify a student's intervention and how to accomplish that. The process for how teachers can prepare to discuss a student whose progress is below expectations and the information needed for the meeting is also included. In addition to providing a vision for a problem-solving meeting, this chapter includes a recommendation of the data that should be discussed at grade-level meetings.

Chapter 7. Referring a Student for Special Education Testing: When the IQ-achievement discrepancy was no longer required for qualification for special education services, it seemed a vacuum was created. What will replace that process? Many states have taken different approaches to address this question. Chapter 7 provides advice on what to bring to a child study meeting and includes data on declines in special education referrals and qualifications after three years of RTI. Recommendations for when and how to communicate with parents are also included.

Additional materials and resources related to *Jumpstart RTI: Using RTI in Your Elementary School Right Now* can be found at http://my.95percentgroup.com/Jumpstart.

1

Ninety-Five Percent of Students at Benchmark Is Achievable

A District Example

As stated in the introduction, this book has a different view of response to intervention (RTI). It looks at RTI as an opportunity to introduce a paradigm shift to a school or district. It's so much more than procedures for special education qualification. RTI can bring increased collaboration among teachers within a building and break down silos between general education and special education. It can change how teachers view students in buildings from "my students" to "our students." RTI is an opportunity to set in place the structures for teachers to talk about students in entirely new ways. It can help teachers put processes in place to implement data-differentiated layers of instruction. The purpose of this chapter is to give readers a peek into the changed place a school building can become. Let's start with the end in mind—a vision for what a district and a school can look like after RTI is fully implemented. Complete definitions of RTI, curriculum-based measurement (CBM), and other terms will be provided in later chapters.

> The purpose of this chapter is to give readers a peek into the changed place a school building can become.

Fifteen years ago in many U.S. elementary schools, classroom teachers were functioning like they existed on their own separate islands. They each prepared and taught their lessons alone, based on their own knowledge and using whatever materials they could access. Teachers held themselves personally responsible for the success of the students assigned to them for the year. There were no reading coaches or professional learning communities to provide the support of colleagues. If one student struggled in learning to read, the teacher could advocate having the child placed in one of the limited number of spots in the one-on-one tutoring program, if offered. If the school received Title I funding, some students were pulled out of the classroom for extra support. Other than these limited forms of support, which were available only in some schools, teachers were on their own to help all students make a year's progress in reading, math, science, and social studies.

Does this sound familiar? The school you taught in at the beginning of your career may not have done it just exactly like this, but most likely you've seen at least some of these practices. A major issue with this approach is that the classroom teacher finds it very hard to address the many different skill needs of the 20 to 30 students in class. Effective intervention groups for most deficit students have only 4 to 5 students at a time. In Grade 1 and above, there are 5 to 10 different types of skill deficits that can hold a student back from proficiently reading grade-level text with comprehension. The teacher can work with only one group at a time and often feels that some of the students are treading water while others are getting instruction.

NEW APPROACH

Given that one of the major problems of past practices is providing small-group instruction that is differentiated by need, let's envision a different approach. What if time is designated in the school's master schedule so that the entire grade-level team provides differentiated instruction for 30 minutes at the same time? Imagine, during a 30-minute block, all students at a grade level go to a small group for differentiated instruction based on deficit skills. This approach, which we've named *walk-to intervention*, is where students walk to where the group is located. The group may meet in the students' own classroom if they have been placed in their classroom teacher's group; however, it's more likely that students will be in a group taught by one of the other classroom teachers or another staff member, such as a reading specialist or teaching assistant. Decisions about the placement of students into groups are based on assessment data, which clearly identifies any skill deficits. The entire grade-level team meets to place students across numerous groups—many more groups than an individual teacher can meet with in a given day. Not only will each teacher at the grade level instruct a group, but each instructional assistant will be trained and supervised to effectively use materials to instruct small intervention groups. This approach is powerful because the number of staff members enables smaller group sizes, instruction is focused on a specific skill, and students can be placed in any of the groups to receive instruction in their skill of greatest need.

Although this model sounds intuitive and logical, there is one cultural issue that stands in the way: This approach involves trust between teachers to "share" students with one another, at least for this half hour daily. For many teachers, sharing their students is not an issue; for others, it poses a problem. Teachers who view themselves as stronger than their colleagues may be hesitant to release students to those they perceive to be weaker in instruction. In addition, educators who feel personally responsible and accountable for their students' achievement may hesitate to give up control. Maybe the approach of the past has caused teachers to feel this way.

One of the most frequent comments I've heard hundreds of schools report is that the language of teachers has changed. It's no longer "my kids"; it's "our kids."

When schools use the walk-to-intervention model, teachers are forced to collaborate because they are placing all their own students across the full range of groups and they are teaching a small group that contains students from any of the classrooms. There is a team effort with this approach, and camaraderie develops. Teachers won't let another teacher skip a day of intervention because it takes all of them to make it happen. One of the most frequent comments I've heard hundreds of schools report is that the language of teachers has changed. It's no longer "my kids"; it's "our kids." This is a very powerful statement because it means that the grade level shares responsibility for all the students.

The walk-to-intervention model solves another issue. One teacher is no longer expected to single-handedly meet all the needs of every one of the students in the classroom. Some teachers are better at teaching phonics, and others are experts in comprehension. Each teacher can elect to teach the skill that takes advantage of personal expertise, and all students can benefit from having access to the expert in that area.

One requirement is that the groups must be different in size. For example, third-grade groups working on multisyllable words may be 14 to 18 students. At the same time, the third-grade students working on short vowels (a skill that should have been mastered by the end of first grade) will be in groups of no more than 5 students, and preferably only 3. Groups working on skills closest to benchmark are larger. Teachers taking the enrichment or acceleration groups must be comfortable having very large groups of 25 to 30 students, which may be larger than a typical classroom. The variability in group size is critical in order to allow the groups working on the lowest skills to be the smallest.

The image of teachers as islands in their own classrooms with doors closed is a thing of the past. With the emphasis on professional learning communities, the practice of reading coaches facilitating curriculum discussions with grade-level teams, and the encouragement of sharing lesson plans, elementary schools have changed dramatically in the past 10 years.

The image of teachers as islands in their own classrooms with doors closed is a thing of the past.

In grade-level collaboration meetings, teachers analyze the lessons and see the bigger picture of how the curriculum progresses throughout the year. Use of skill continuums clarify what students should master by the end of each grade. For example, in kindergarten, students need to master all levels of the phonological awareness continuum. That includes not only working with syllables and onset-rimes but also isolating, segmenting, blending, and manipulating phonemes. If a student hasn't mastered the skills through the core program, then placement in an intervention group provides access to more-explicit instruction on a deficit skill that should have already been mastered. Teachers use CBMs as well as diagnostic assessments to determine whether a student has mastered or is deficient in each skill.

By having a system of expected skill mastery, the school can be preventive and intervene as soon as a student begins to fall behind.

By having a system of expected skill mastery, the school can be preventive and intervene as soon as a student begins to fall behind. First-grade teachers can rely on the kindergarten teachers to have been proactive in intervening to address any phonological awareness skill deficits. In schools in which students move between schools within the district, teachers can count on students arriving with mastery of particular skills. When there is a districtwide adoption of a common set of assessments and data-management systems, teachers can instantly access a student's data without waiting to receive a paper file from the student's previous teacher.

Data is used not only to initially identify any skill deficits and place students in a group for intervention but also to track whether instruction is working. Periodic, scheduled progress monitoring enables teachers to track a student's gains. If the instruction is not producing measurable results, teachers have to change course and try something else. A prevention approach with periodic progress monitoring communicates urgency. The entire staff understands the importance of moving students through the skills continuum on time and not allowing any extra time to go by.

WHAT LEVEL OF SUCCESS IS POSSIBLE?

Having read this "new approach," educators should ask for evidence that the effort required to put these RTI practices in place will be worth it. Nearly all states recommend or require that schools use RTI data when determining which students qualify for special education services. The objective behind this is to replace or enhance the previous qualification procedure; IQ-achievement discrepancies were used to show that a student has the capability to learn yet has not been successful in learning—and the reason for the lack of success is a specific learning disability.

While nearly all states recommend implementation of RTI, most have provided districts very limited guidance or specificity on *how* to implement it. We believe that schools should implement RTI because it's the right thing to do for students, not just the required thing to do. And while you're doing it, you might as well proceed in a manner that puts collaboration in place, something that many principals are trying to embed in their school's culture.

As stated previously, it's important to start with the end in mind. What should we be striving for? Let's look at an example of a medium-sized U.S. school district and what it did to implement RTI. This is a story about taking an RTI implementation to scale in a reasonably sized district. RTI created a new paradigm that will continue long after individual champions are gone; this district built capacity of its staff so that differentiated instruction will be sustained.

RTI created a new paradigm that will continue long after individual champions are gone; this district built capacity of its staff so that differentiated instruction will be sustained.

As a quick overview of the district's results (more details will be provided later in this chapter), I'll outline the achievements during five years focused on raising reading-achievement scores districtwide. The district's investment paid off as evident by these key indicators in the fall of 2009:

1. Because of interventions with kindergarten students, 94% of the district's 4,300 Grade 1 students entered at benchmark as measured by *DIBELS* (*Dynamic Indicators of Basic Early Literacy Skills*, Good & Kaminski, 2002b), which is up from 84% five years ago.

2. Because of interventions with Grade 1 students, 88% of the district's students entered Grade 2 at *DIBELS* benchmark, which is up from 79% five years earlier.

3. On the spring 2009 state assessment, the district was first in Grade 3 reading scores among the 17 largest districts in the state.

Description of Example District

The elementary curriculum coordinator describes her district as "a data-driven district where reading is Goal Number 1 in our strategic plan." The district is located in a community about 30 minutes outside of a major city. Because districts in this particular state are county-wide, this district's 38 elementary schools serve both high and low SES (socioeconomic status) schools. Eight of the elementary schools received Reading First funding, and currently fourteen receive Title I schoolwide funds. (Both Reading First and Title I are U.S. Department of Education programs designed to provide funding for improving achievement of students from lower-income families.) Although 34% of the students districtwide receive free and reduced lunch, that population tends to be concentrated primarily in about a dozen schools in which 90% of students receive free lunch. In spite of the fact that students are from 148 countries and speak 108 languages, the percentage of students considered ELL (English language learners) is smaller than in many U.S. districts. The teachers' union is very active in the district. Fifteen of the buildings aren't eligible for either Reading First or Title I funds, so they don't receive the money and materials that the other buildings do.

How Did the District Do It?

This district implemented a multitiered model of reading intervention districtwide for kindergarten through Grade 2 starting in 2004. As of early 2010, 30 of 38 elementary buildings have participated in on-site implementation and coaching to aid implementation of RTI. The district wants all schools to provide high-quality instruction and to achieve high reading levels. The district partnered with my consulting company, 95 Percent Group, to provide job-embedded, sustained professional development rich in coaching and support. Instead of the one-shot workshop model, the district knew that to make gains it would need a site-based approach where teachers were taught to analyze student data at a level far deeper than just the score, place students in groups focused by skill deficits, and practice effective small-group instructional strategies. Teachers were provided time to absorb the true meaning of data-differentiated instruction under the guidance of experts.

The district's K–12 Reading Plan, required by the state department of education, provided the structure for this process. According to one of the staff members, the state is "requesting and highly encouraging us to assess with *DIBELS*. We are not going to give the *DIBELS* three times a year to all students and not

> The mantra was that if we are going to gather all this assessment data, then we need to know what it means.

know what the red, yellow, and green colors mean." The mantra was that if we are going to gather all this assessment data, then we need to know what it means.

The district's K–12 Reading Plan articulates a set of decision rules that guide assessment and data-analysis practices in schools. Teachers were taught not to assume that all skills are mastered just because the child's *DIBELS* instructional recommendation level is benchmark; only after looking at the probes to confirm that accuracy is above 95% do teachers place students in an acceleration or enrichment group. If accuracy is below 95%, teachers dig deeper into the data to determine whether to assess with our phonological awareness or phonics diagnostic screener.

As the elementary curriculum coordinator said, "One of the main principles that drove the district's RTI implementation was a goal to level the playing field across our schools." One of my strongest memories when I first started working with this district five years ago was listening to the elementary curriculum coordinator say at an administrators' meeting that "we are all reading *first* schools." In spite of the fact that only a small percentage of the schools qualified and received federal Reading First funds, the view was that there were children not reading well in *all* the schools, including the high-performing schools—just not as many. Therefore, good reading practices needed to be in place uniformly throughout all the district's schools. The goal was that, as much as possible, all teachers receive the training that the reading coaches and teachers got; the district committed professional development funds to cover training to the extent possible. Although a reading coach position wasn't funded in every building, a "literacy team member" was designated, who attended monthly full-day trainings.

Phase-In: How the District Moved Across the Buildings

The district made an important strategic decision that contributed to its success—it would go slow and get it right. It didn't try to implement RTI at all buildings in the first year; it didn't even implement it at all grade levels in the selected buildings in the first year. Instead, four years have been spent providing professional development and assistance to 30 of the 38 elementary buildings in this gradual phase-in process. When supporting a new cadre of schools, professional development was provided in strands according to role. Administrators met quarterly during all four years, and monthly meetings were held with one designated reading specialist from each building throughout the first three years of RTI implementation. This one

> The district made an important strategic decision that contributed to its success–it would go slow and get it right.

designated literacy team member from each building was, in some cases, a full-time reading coach and, in other cases, a person who taught small groups of struggling readers.

Knowing that the one-shot workshop approach doesn't result in implementation with something this complex, the district used a sustained job-embedded approach to professional development. It worked through cadres of four to eight schools a year to provide yearlong assistance for the kindergarten and first-grade staff the initial year. All kindergarten through Grade 1 classroom teachers attended a full-day workshop, plus the grade-level teams met in school-based modeling and coaching sessions with a 95 Percent Group consultant several times during the year. The on-site sessions with the consultant focused on making sure that the assessment data were used: Students below benchmark on their *DIBELS* scores got 30 minutes daily in a targeted skills group where effective instructional strategies were employed.

Funding provided through Reading First actually provided the start to this implementation even before it was referred to as RTI. Some schools took full advantage of this opportunity and others didn't. When the elementary curriculum coordinator observed the professional development and listened to the positive feedback, she realized the potential of this approach for the entire district. She recommended allocating district professional development (PD) funds to make this same approach available to other schools but knew that to be successful the plan would have to get the attention and commitment of a school team. After several hours of strategizing, we created a plan that would use an application process to select schools that seemed committed to implementation. The district decided that the only schools that were eligible to apply the first year were those that didn't receive either Reading First or Title I funding.

In March 2006, the elementary curriculum coordinator went to a principals' meeting to present this opportunity. Eligible schools could return to their buildings and work with their literacy teams to prepare a submission. Interested schools would complete applications to participate in district-funded PD as a demonstration site (demo site). The selected sites would receive a year of "free" (district-funded), sustained professional development, a few extra materials, and attention from the district office. The application was simple and included only three questions about the school's commitment to use data to inform decisions, and responses were limited to three pages plus a graph of the school's data. There was enough funding to select four schools to participate as demo sites in the initial year. In return, the schools would be asked to allow staff from other schools to observe.

Yet perhaps the most important thing the demo sites received was less tangible; embracing this initiative gave the staff a focus and vision,

Embracing this initiative gave the staff a focus and vision, and the collaboration time with staff from the other demo sites provided a professional learning community with access to models from other buildings.

and the collaboration time with staff from the other demo sites provided a professional learning community with access to models from other buildings. During the year, consultants instructed, observed, coached, and mentored the teachers. The result was that the teachers and reading specialists in the demo sites improved their decision-making capabilities. They developed skills in interpreting their students' data, making informed grouping decisions, and teaching small intervention groups using more-effective strategies. They came to student study teams with individual progress-monitoring folders.

One of the four demo site principals reported, "In 2006, when I became principal, 64% of kindergarten students met *DIBELS* benchmark levels. Two years later, 88% of this same group of students started second grade at grade level in reading."

Going to Scale: Offering Similar Support to *All* Schools

The district's goal was for all 38 buildings to use the processes and practices so that all students reached reading goals and 95% or more of students would reach benchmark reading levels. In order to go to scale with all 38 elementary buildings, the plan was to provide assistance to each school to the degree needed to achieve implementation. Because of success during the first year, the district decided to provide some support, albeit more limited than the previous year, so the demo sites could not only deepen implementation at kindergarten through Grade 1 but also expand the intervention groups to Grades 2 and 3. In addition, the program was expanded to take on another cadre of five schools named Spotlight I schools. They received the same type of professional development, including the teacher workshop and on-site data analysis and instructional coaching. The third year, the demo sites had embedded practices in kindergarten through Grade 3 and, therefore, the only support they needed was literacy-team and administrator support to sustain the implementation. Next, a third cadre of six schools was accepted through applications again, this time called Spotlight II schools (see Table 1.1).

There are several benefits of the district's use of phasing in groups of schools for the intensive professional development. This enabled the district to concentrate funds to provide extensive support for kindergarten and first-grade teachers to learn new data-analysis and instructional techniques. It also allowed schools to learn from their mistakes. One of the Spotlight I schools tried to implement across kindergarten through Grade 5 in its first year even though the district PD

Table 1.1 Schools in the District

Site-Based Coaching	2005–2006	2006–2007	2007–2008	2008–2009	2009–2010
Reading First Schools	Eight schools in their fourth year of Reading First funding in 2005–2006				
Grades K–1	X	X			
Grades 2–3	X	X			
Demo Sites	Four schools selected by application process				
Grades K–1		X	X limited		
Grades 2–3			X		
Spotlight I	Five schools selected by application process				
Grades K–1			X	X limited	
Grades 2–3				X	
Spotlight II	Six schools selected by application process				
Grades K–1				X	X limited
Grades 2–3					X
Title I Schools	Twelve of the fourteen schools that are receiving Title I funding, not selected by application process				
Grades K–1					X
Grades 2–3					

was for kindergarten and Grade 1 only. That turned out to be a mistake as later reported by both the principal and the reading coach. The stress in the building reached a very high level; it was just too much to take on in a single year. At administrator meetings in later years, the principal shared that she would not encourage anyone to do what she tried to do.

All buildings sent a representative to attend the administrators' and coaches' training, and some of the schools took advantage of the offers to observe at the demo sites and spotlight schools. Most of the teams who visited took the assessment practices, data-analysis and grouping procedures, and intervention instructional practices to their buildings. One of the Spotlight I reading coaches remarked, "Everyone would come and watch the process—board members, district office staff, other teachers, and coaches from other schools." Visitors came to see key activities, such as grade-level meetings to regroup students with fresh progress-monitoring data. They would observe teachers at a grade level bringing filled-out sticky notes to designate the next skill needed for each student. Using a science project board, teachers placed sticky notes under skill categories and then arranged the names in groups once they could see how many students needed each skill. The final step was to assign teachers to groups, and by the conclusion of the 40-minute meeting, the grouping and staffing were done.

Many of the Spotlight I and II school staff members had visited the demo sites, so they were much more informed about the commitment involved. As a result, their readiness to implement was much higher than the demo sites. A reading specialist at one of the Spotlight I schools said that when she went to visit a demo site, she had been doing pull-out groups and seeing more than 100 students daily. However, that wasn't enough. She just couldn't reach all the students that needed small-group intervention instruction. After the two years of PD provided to her school as a Spotlight II school, a major shift occurred; the classroom teachers are now providing small-group intervention instruction. Although the reading specialist still sees students, she is no longer the only one working with students who are below benchmark. Her school calls the differentiation time "surf time" to give it a more neutral name than "intervention time," because students who are at benchmark level are receiving acceleration instruction while students who are below benchmark focus on addressing skill deficits. Now that the teachers understand the process and have bought into it with the support of a committed principal, the reading specialist updates groups after each progress-monitoring period via spreadsheets posted on the school's server. One impact that this reading specialist commented on recently is that now teachers are saying, "It's not your kids and my kids, it's our kids. This works—my kids are moving." In the spring of 2009, her school was the leader in third-grade reading scores for the district on the state assessment.

Many of the Spotlight I and II school staff members had visited the demo sites, so they were much more informed about the commitment involved. As a result, their readiness to implement was much higher than the demo sites.

District Role in Implementation

After the success of the demo sites, the district office mandated several critical things. First, the elementary schools were required to add a 30-minute intervention block outside of the 90-minute reading block. In addition, the district recommended that schools use the walk-to-intervention approach, in which students are grouped across grade levels. Principals were encouraged to realign instructional personnel to increase the number of staff members available to provide differentiated group instruction. Schedules were carefully examined to free up assistants who were doing bus and lunch duty so that they now could be available during differentiation block times. These assistants were critical to making group sizes smaller.

In addition to mandating that elementary schools add intervention blocks to their master schedules, the district office specified the assessments that would be used for elementary students. All K–5 students were assessed with *DIBELS* (this was before the state's early literacy assessment was available). The district provided training on how to give the assessment, as well as how to use the data-management system for collecting and reporting the data. To standardize diagnostic assessments, the district acquired licenses for 95 Percent Group's diagnostic screeners (*PSI*, or *Phonics Screener for Intervention*, and *PASI*, or *Phonological Awareness Screener for Intervention*) for all elementary buildings. It also developed a process where every student who scores below benchmark now has an intervention folder that accompanies the student when moving to another district school. This solved the issue of having to wait for a cumulative folder to be sent when a student transferred from one school to another. These intervention folders hold the scoring forms for the phonological awareness and phonics diagnostic screeners, so the receiving teacher can see the most recent progress-monitoring scores and place the student in an intervention group immediately.

Data to Validate Success

After five years, this district has 95% of students at benchmark in kindergarten and Grade 1 and is approaching 95% at Grade 2. Improvement during the last five years, districtwide, in *DIBELS* scores (18,000 K–3 students) is shown in Table 1.2.

As Table 1.2 shows, in five years, this district has made tremendous progress. Because of the excellent interventions in kindergarten, the first-grade students are entering the year with much stronger skills; the

Table 1.2 Districtwide *DIBELS* Data: Five-Year Change Based on Beginning-of-Year Measurements

Grade	Five-Year Change Students at Benchmark	Five-Year Change Students at Intensive
Grade 1	84% to 94%	4% to 1%
Grade 2	74% to 88%	8% to 4%
Grade 3	46% to 75%	26% to 9%

beginning-of-year first-grade scores have gone from 84% to 94% of students at benchmark in *DIBELS*. This figure includes data from all 38 elementary schools and represents approximately 4,000 students at each grade level. This is clearly a model of "going to scale."

In addition, in the past, there used to be discussions about a "second-grade slump" in the district. Staff believed that students would finish a wonderful first-grade year and then slump in second grade. Many reasons were offered to explain this decline in reading scores, including that the assessment passages were too hard, that the passages were too focused on expository to the exclusion of narrative, and even that second grade is where principals place the weakest teachers. The results in Table 1.2 show that the second-grade slump had actually been a first-grade hangover. Students didn't get caught up in first grade, and their deficits just became more obvious in second grade.

Tier I Core-Program Implementation

The district uses one of the big Tier I basal reading programs; however, it is now about seven years old. The district has done as much as any other reasonably sized district to implement the core program with fidelity. One of the critical things the district did to assure that Tier I would be as effective as possible was to align the core with the continuum of skills for phonological awareness and phonics used in the RTI implementation. The phonological awareness (PA) continuum represents a progression approach to articulating a student's development of PA skills from simple to complex. Therefore, the skill continuums for Tiers I, II, and III are the same, which provides a consistent learning-to-read continuum across grade levels. The district believes that this gave them one solidified approach to instruction. In kindergarten, for example, a committee of teachers and reading specialists examined all the lessons in the core basal reading program and made charts to show whether there are lessons on each skill in the phonological awareness continuum.

In addition to the curriculum mapping of the core program to the skills continuums, the committee also created a kindergarten toolbox. Each kindergarten teacher received a box with materials to use when teaching the skills so that the core was supplemented to address identified weaknesses.

Some RTI advisers recommend taking a full year to study the Tier I core program to understand the degree to which it meets the needs of the district's student population and identify any supplemental materials needed. This step is critical—if the core is failing to meet the needs of too many students, then too many students will need Tier II intervention instruction. Within this particular state, the RTI training recommends this step. However, the district launched its RTI effort before the state released its training. The approach the district took was that it couldn't afford to spend an entire year studying the Tier I core first; it would implement Tier II and study Tier I simultaneously. As stated by one of the administrators, "Frankly, we don't have time to do that."

> We recommend to all our clients this process of evaluating and addressing the shortcomings of Tier I curriculum while simultaneously initiating Tier II small groups.

We recommend to all our clients this process of evaluating and addressing the shortcomings of Tier I curriculum while simultaneously initiating Tier II small groups. Implementing the data-analysis and grouping techniques discussed in Chapter 3 of this book equips the staff to better analyze why Tier I is not effective and determine beneficial supplements or strategies to address the deficits.

PROFESSIONAL DEVELOPMENT

Many times when district reading scores demonstrate huge gains, one of the first questions neighboring districts ask is "What program are you using?" This is the wrong question to ask. Scientifically based research studies using random assignment of students to different published programs have demonstrated that there is nearly no difference in student results among several of the major published basal reading programs. Success is not about which program you buy; it's about how you train your teachers to deliver excellent instruction using the materials available. So the question that the neighboring districts should ask is "What was your professional development model?"

> Success is not about which program you buy; it's about how you train your teachers to deliver excellent instruction using the materials available.

The district's approach to professional development provided different training for principals, APs (assistant principals), coaches, teachers, and so on. Implementing data-driven differentiated instruction in an elementary school is very hard without the support of the principal. Since the principal needs to be on board, it's wise to start the implementation by planning a principals' meeting. But it doesn't stop there. We recommend continuing to meet with principals regularly, especially during the first year of an implementation. Principals benefit from having their own meetings where they not only receive information but also share challenges and advice with one another. In addition, in districts where most of the elementary buildings have assistant principals, we plan morning meetings with principals and a repeat of the same content with APs in the afternoon. Although principals don't need to analyze data at the student level, they need to know what teachers are supposed to be looking at when forming their groups effectively and how to read the data reports. The district provided training with a consultant quarterly for the first two years, and then, as each cadre went through on-site intensive coaching, that smaller group of principals met regularly as well.

Reading coaches or RTI coordinators also need training focused on their needs. Their role positions them as the local expert in the building, so they need to be able to advise the principal as well as support teachers. Many principals meet weekly with the RTI coordinator to discuss implementation, talk about processes, problem solve issues within grade-level teams, and generally keep the implementation going. In the 70% of schools in the district that didn't have a full-time reading coach, a reading expert, who was referred to as the literacy team member, was designated. The literacy team member met for one full day a month the first year the district launched RTI, and a consultant was there about half of those times while the elementary curriculum coordinator facilitated discussion and sharing during the other meetings. These schools also received more summer training for several days during the first two summers. As each building went through its two-year cycle of site-based modeling and coaching, the literacy team members had sustained training not only by attending each grade level's meeting with the consultant but also by attending a separate strand of meetings designed to pretrain them in the instructional strategies that would be provided to teachers.

Administrator Training

The district's view was that to be effective at leading the RTI implementation in their building, principals needed several different types of information. The professional development provided to all administrators included how to

- schedule time for differentiated instruction;
- allocate staff resources to enable appropriate-sized groups;
- use the PA and phonics continuums to consider student-skill mastery;
- discuss data and review reports from *DIBELS* and diagnostic screeners; and
- observe intervention group instruction and identify when teacher support is needed.

Principals make several key structural decisions mostly in the area of scheduling and staffing. These decisions are important because they have a direct effect on the number of minutes of instruction students receive in their differentiated groups.

In April 2006, at the end of the first year of the demo sites implementation, the district held an important meeting with the principals of all 38 elementary schools. The purpose of this meeting was to communicate a recommendation that each building add to its master schedule a designated 30-minute differentiation block outside of the core reading-block time. Demo site schools had done this and had learned that it was a critical component of their implementation. During this spring meeting, principals heard about the advantages the demo sites had because of their common grade-level intervention blocks for kindergarten and first grade. The intervention blocks enabled the demo sites to group across classrooms and "flood" all available staff to join teachers in teaching intervention groups at those two grade levels to reduce group sizes. After this spring meeting, approximately half of the schools voluntarily added the intervention blocks for the next fall. In later years, the district added this to its K–12 Reading Plan, making the intervention block a requirement for all schools.

In the educational community, there is much discussion about the role of the principal as an instructional leader. Overseeing an elementary building is very difficult if a principal doesn't have a basic understanding of reading instruction. Therefore, one of the most important yet difficult skills for principals to acquire is the ability to walk through classrooms and recognize whether the instruction is effective or needs improvement. The district's professional development plan addressed this in a powerful way. While a school participated in the site-based implementation support, the principal received training in how to use a "walk-through observation" form to identify whether characteristics of effective intervention instruction were present or absent. During the walk-through training, which occurred at one of the buildings, the group of principals all observed the same instruction, took notes on their observation forms, and then debriefed on which aspects of instruction were excellent and which needed coaching.

Although this training was focused on intervention instruction, much of the discussion applied to delivering effective reading instruction during the core as well.

As the elementary curriculum coordinator said, "It's hard for building administrators to inspect what they don't know." Principals need to trust their reading coaches, but it's tempting to defer too much to the judgment of the coach rather than to judge instruction themselves. While it's beneficial to have coaches play a key role in identifying good and poor examples of instruction, principals who know what to look for are better instructional leaders. I recall one conversation that happened after such training. At the conclusion of a walk-through observation training, the principal of the host school lingered in the conference room. After everyone else left, she looked at me and said, "I learned so much today. I didn't know what to look for. I also realized that my reading coach knows a lot. She leaned over while we were watching a teacher and told me what was wrong, and it was exactly what you said later in the debriefing."

While it's beneficial to have coaches play a key role in identifying good and poor examples of instruction, principals who know what to look for are better instructional leaders.

Principals were also trained on how to track student progress. Not only did they use *DIBELS* reports, but also they were given reports that show indicators to track data monthly using consolidated diagnostic screener progress-monitoring data. They were provided with reports to track the rate of movement of students up either the phonological awareness or the phonics continuum, depending on the grade level.

Reading Coach and Reading Specialist Training

All the literacy team representatives participated in monthly meetings for several years, as well as in two summer institutes. Some of the meetings focused on foundational knowledge about reading development. The topics at the meetings included information about how to

- analyze *DIBELS* data to determine which students needed further diagnostic assessment to pinpoint skill deficits;
- administer and score PA and phonics diagnostic screeners;
- place students who score below benchmark in small groups based on skill deficits identified by the diagnostic screeners;
- help teachers plan and deliver effective intervention instruction; and
- watch the progress of individual students monthly and move students up the continuum in groups once they show mastery through assessment with alternate forms of the diagnostic screener.

Teacher Training

When a school entered a cadre, classroom teachers of the designated grade levels (usually only kindergarten and Grade 1 in the first year) were provided with special training for two years. The first step of this training is for teachers to attend one full-day workshop by grade level followed by four grade-level meetings in each school, typically a half day each. Throughout the year, teachers were taught how to

- analyze *DIBELS* data to determine which students needed further diagnostic assessment to pinpoint skill deficits;
- administer and score PA and phonics screeners;
- place students who score below benchmark in small groups based on skill deficits identified by the diagnostic screeners;
- watch the progress of individual students monthly and move students up the continuum in groups once they show mastery through assessment with alternate forms of the diagnostic screener; and
- teach using routines for phonological awareness and phonics instruction.

The district provided some intervention materials, but the focus was much more about learning the format of an intervention lesson and how to incorporate instructional strategies and routines that are powerful for struggling readers. Teachers were given support in learning the look and feel of effective intervention instruction and given Routine Cards[1] to assist them in learning the foundational strategies such as "move it and say it" to teach phoneme segmentation. Before this professional development, teachers had been using activities they had downloaded from a reading-research website as the core of their lesson. What changed is that the teachers' lessons incorporated routines to provide good explicit instruction in the target skill, and the focus of the activities shifted to providing practice on what was previously taught. Teachers mastered the routines by not only watching the consultant model "live" with their students during visits to the school but also by viewing online videos of each routine "just in time"—right before they taught it.

Teachers mastered the routines by not only watching the consultant model "live" with their students during visits to the school but also by viewing online videos of each routine "just in time"–right before they taught it.

NEXT STEPS

Having achieved substantial progress in the kindergarten through Grade 3 reading scores during the past five years, the district's next step is to move on to Grades 4 and 5. There are many students currently in fourth and fifth grade who didn't get the benefit of early identification and immediate intervention when they were in kindergarten through third grade. In addition, the fourth- and fifth-grade teachers haven't received the same model of professional development. Addressing reading deficits is much more challenging at these grade levels. The district is aware that while some students have decoding deficits, others will need intervention in comprehension. The district has already begun using the phonics screener to identify and sort students based on whether they have decoding issues versus whether they decode well but have vocabulary and comprehension deficits that suppress their ability to process what they are reading. Through assessing a sample of fourth-grade students with the *PSI*, the district found a significant percentage of struggling readers cannot differentiate words with long vowel silent-*e* versus the consonant-vowel-consonant pattern.

While presenting at a conference in November 2009, the district's elementary curriculum coordinator stated, "It's our commitment to

---

[1] *Blueprint for Intervention: Routine Cards and Guide*, published by 95 Percent Group Inc. (2008).

bring fourth grade to 90%." This district will face what others we've worked with in the past have experienced: The challenge at these grade levels is much greater than in the earlier grade levels. It's not just that the students didn't get the benefit of early intervention. It's also because the intermediate elementary teachers believe they teach content not phonics or phonological awareness. Unless teachers taught a lower grade level earlier in their career, many later grade teachers don't know how to teach reading. Many have never been trained in the syllable types and how to teach students to use them to break apart words they can't read by sight.

Reflection on Successes

The district office is driven for student results and continuous improvements. Although already viewed as high performing, the district recognized that there were pockets of low achievement when it started this process. As the assistant superintendent said, "Are we proud of where we are? Yes. Are we where we want to be? No." The district is very excited about its progress, and it should be. What's great about working with this district is that it is committed to sticking with the plan. The district also is receptive to suggestions and stays focused on what the data shows is working.

Several key messages from this district's story follow:

- Be true to the data. Make decisions about schools and students based on data.
- Maintain fidelity to the model. Find a model of implementation that works and stick with it. If a school wants district support, it needs to implement the model with fidelity.
- Go slow to go fast. Support buildings to get it right at kindergarten and Grade 1 before moving up the grade levels in a building.
- Standardize assessment and structural components across a district:
    - Designate assessment instruments for the entire district.
    - Use diagnostic screeners in concert with the CBM.
    - Require schools to have 30-minute intervention blocks.
    - Use the walk-to-intervention model for the collaboration benefits it brings.
- Expect high results.

Having watched this implementation for five years, I saw many benefits of what the district achieved beyond the success in the numbers. It's clear that the district has built teacher capacity on how to look at student data, pinpoint deficit skills, and monitor students' acquisition of deficit skills along continuums. More significantly, the district has built this capacity across nearly all of the 38 buildings. But what's perhaps most striking is what's been accomplished on other dimensions. Teachers talk about "our kids" instead of "my kids." The grade-level teams collaborate in ways that they didn't before RTI. This shared dialogue about students and teaching is the end goal of what's embodied in the popular term *professional learning communities*. The district knows more about reading development than it did five years ago and understands how to look at a student and figure out *why* he can't read on grade level. Teachers have a path to follow when a student is not where she should be. There's no more guessing; teachers are confident about what to do. As the director of reading said at a conference presentation, "We've changed so much in the last four years, we hardly recognize ourselves." This is the potential of effective school improvement under the umbrella of response to intervention.

CONCLUSION

Chapter 1 focused on starting with the end in mind and provided a description of a district that is five years into their RTI implementation. Not only have they reached 95% of students at benchmark in single schools, but they have successfully reached this student-achievement goal on average across the district's 38 elementary schools at several grade levels. The district's story provides not only tips for implementing but also motivation for those who are newer to the process.

Additional materials and resources related to *Jumpstart RTI: Using RTI in Your Elementary School Right Now* can be found at http://my.95percentgroup.com/Jumpstart.

2

Getting Ready

Hearing about the successes of the district discussed in Chapter 1, which used RTI as a school-reform effort, most schools and districts ask, "How did they do it?" Nearly all schools start the process of implementing RTI with some overview presentations about what it is. One important reason to have an overview session is to develop a common understanding of RTI and its terminology. There are numerous terms associated with RTI, and many books and articles define these terms differently. For example, in some locations, *Tier III* is special education and, in other locations, it's intervention before qualification. In most cases, RTI stands for response to intervention, but in a few locations, it's response to instruction. The definition of RTI used in this book follows:

> *Response to intervention* is a dynamic problem-solving process in which data is integral in making decisions about which skills struggling readers lack and whether intervention instruction provided to date has been effective.

Response to intervention: A dynamic problem-solving process in which data is integral in making decisions about which skills struggling readers lack and whether intervention instruction provided to date has been effective.

Implementation of response to intervention in a school revolves around an understanding of and commitment to a set of beliefs about students and early reading. Five of these fundamental beliefs follow:

1. Preventive action is better than the wait-to-fail approach.
2. Early intervention is more effective than later remediation.

3. Universal screening helps to avoid students falling through the cracks.
4. Tiers of instruction are available to meet the needs of all students.
5. Data is used to pinpoint deficit skills and to determine whether instruction is working.

To build a common language and a basic level of understanding about RTI, consider using a publication by the National Association of State Directors of Special Education (NASDSE) titled *Response to Intervention: Policy Considerations and Implementation* (Batsche et al., 2006). This publication includes eight fundamental principles about RTI, as shown in Table 2.1.

Throughout this book, we'll use a framework for considering how to implement RTI in reading in an elementary building. This framework will be referred to as *implementation at the school level* and will describe the process in terms of planning, creating structures, and developing processes that are typically in place in schools that use RTI (Figure 2.1).

Many RTI experts recommend completing an extensive planning process before launching RTI. While planning is beneficial, momentum is lost if it's composed of too many unnecessary forms and extended over too long a period of time. On the other hand, too often schools "jump first

Table 2.1 Eight Core Principles of Response to Intervention

I	We can effectively teach all children.
II	Intervene early.
III	Use a multitier model of service delivery.
IV	Use a problem-solving model to make decisions within a multitier model.
V	Use scientific, research-based, validated intervention and instruction to the extent available.
VI	Monitor student progress to inform instruction.
VII	Use data to make decisions. A data-based decision regarding student response to intervention is central to RTI practices.
VIII	Use assessment for screening, diagnostics, and progress monitoring.

Source: From Batsche et al. (2006), pp. 19–20.

Figure 2.1 Implementation at the School Level

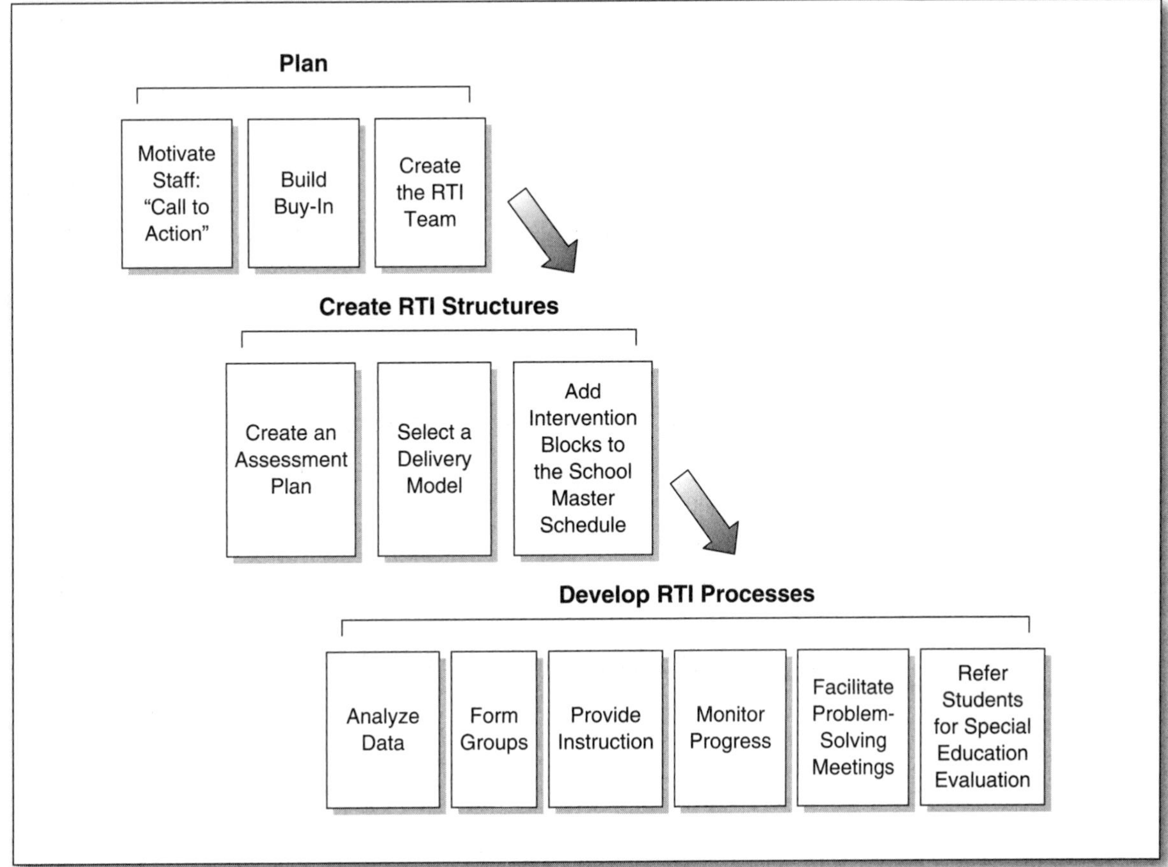

and plan later"; they start doing activities without considering their goals and the big picture and ignore the interrelationships of their actions. When it comes to planning, the "Goldilocks principle" is appropriate: Not too much. Not too little. Just right.

What are the most important things that need to happen in the planning stage? (1) Motivate staff: "call to action," (2) build buy-in, and (3) create the RTI team (see Figure 2.2).

The purpose of this chapter is to describe how to get ready at the school level. The central focus of the planning stage is about motivating and obtaining buy-in from the school's staff members and developing a leadership team. While it's tempting to skip this stage, keep in mind that what you do during the planning stage impacts the implementation for years to come, especially the ultimate buy-in of the staff. It's not about filling out various planning and self-evaluation forms; it's about strategizing and doing what it takes for staff to be motivated to put new processes in place. You'll know you're ready to move on when the leadership team has been formed and the staff is coming around.

Figure 2.2 Planning Stage

Plan

Motivate Staff: "Call to Action"	Build Buy-In	Create the RTI Team

• Complete CBM to attain benchmark baseline data
• Identify two to three data talking points for *why* RTI is imperative for your school
• Repeat data talking points often
• Show your commitment to RTI by attending critical professional development
	• Attend at least one grade-level team meeting to dialogue about RTI and answer questions
	• Meet individually with teachers who may be reluctant or resistant
	• Commit to provide support for teachers (release time for planning, budget for needed materials, etc.)
	• Celebrate incremental improvements
		• **Create a School RTI Team**
		  • Assistant Principal, Reading Coach, Title I Coordinator, Special Education Coordinator, Grade-Level Team Representatives, School Psychologist, Speech-Language Pathologist
		• **Appoint an RTI Coordinator**
		  • Evaluate skills of possible candidates compared to job description
		  • Name an RTI coordinator
		  • Define the position
		  • Inform staff of the role of the RTI coordinator

MOTIVATE STAFF: "CALL TO ACTION"

One goal of the planning stage is to motivate staff to *want* to do RTI. Motivating is an important part of initiating RTI in your building. It's imperative that everyone in the building knows why you are doing RTI. It's not about saying, "We have to do RTI"—that won't get you very far. When anyone is told they *have* to do something that they don't believe in, it's unlikely that they'll put their heart into it. Teachers will need to change some processes for RTI to be successful; it's more work, especially at first. Teachers will come on board more readily if they see and believe in the need for change (see Figure 2.3).

FIgure 2.3 Motivate Staff: "Call to Action"

- Complete CBM to attain benchmark baseline data
- Identify two to three data talking points for *why* RTI is imperative for your school
- Repeat data talking points often
- Show your commitment to RTI by attending critical professional development

Complete Benchmark Curriculum-Based Measurement Data

Think about what it would take for your school to take action. What would make teachers want to do things differently? One Illinois district collected CBM data for all students in the district from kindergarten through eighth grade. They found that more than half of the middle school students were reading below grade level on the oral reading fluency (ORF) measures. While this data confirmed the intuition of many middle school teachers, it also had the effect of shocking the entire district into action. Elementary principals talked about how reading instruction at the elementary schools *had* to change in order to improve the reading outcomes for middle school students in the future.

Because one of the most effective ways to call teachers to action is through data, collecting baseline data is an important initial step.

Because one of the most effective ways to call teachers to action is through data, collecting baseline data is an important initial step. By collecting data before the school starts implementing RTI, you'll be able to track improvements over time and compare the percentage of students reading at benchmark before and after implementation. Schools typically use a data management reporting system, such as those offered by the authors of *DIBELS* or *AIMSweb* (NCS Pearson, available at http://www.aimsweb.com, 2010), for their baseline data, and by continuing to assess students periodically, they are able to measure improvements. Although most schools collect many other types of data, CBM data is a critical part of RTI and other data cannot fulfill the same purpose. Sometimes schools ask whether they need to assess with CBMs or if their reading inventory data, such as *DRA* (*Developmental Reading Assessment*, 2005), will work. While determining the reading level for each student is helpful, the purpose is different. CBMs are necessary because they meet the following objectives:

- They assess an individual student's proficiency in a skill (reading) against a nationally named benchmark.
- They take a minimal amount of time to administer (fewer than 10 minutes per student).
- The data measures progress over time through repeated assessment with alternate forms.
- They allow for the consolidation of data by student, classroom, school, and district and for comparison of scores over time.

Identify Data Talking Points

Identify two to three data points that will call the staff to action. In this book, these points will be called *data talking points*. After the baseline data is collected, assemble the building's administrative team (including teacher representatives) to analyze the data. Challenge this group to determine whether the school can be proud of this data. Ask them to identify any areas that they are not proud of, or things that really bother them about the data. We recommend doing this at the school level because, although teachers care about their district, they identify most with their own building. Limit the number of data talking points to two or three and make them memorable.

The team should write down these two or three data talking points and their insights from analyzing the school's data. Examples of good data talking points follow:

- Two-thirds of first-grade students are not reading at grade level at year-end.
- Having 18% of our students on individual education plans (IEPs) for reading difficulty is unacceptably high.
- Because 10% more second-grade students fail to reach benchmark at year-end versus the beginning of the year, second grade must be a priority this year.
- It is unacceptable that African American students underperform the Caucasian population by 30%.

Repeat Data Talking Points Often

Now that you have the data talking points, think about how to repeat them often enough so that every teacher will be able to name at least two of them. Integrate the data talking points into comments; for example, "The work that's been done this month assessing students is terrific. I really think it's going to help us overcome that second-grade slump, where our students lose 10% of the gains we make in Grade 1."

Why do this? Sometimes there are teachers who think, "Our reading scores are OK; we are doing fine." If you have taken time to discuss the data talking points, then it takes the wind out of the sails of the naysayers who claim that change isn't needed because they think everything is fine just the way it is. Principals should constantly "take the school's pulse" to determine how well the implementation is going and to be aware of issues as they arise.

Principals should constantly "take the school's pulse" to determine how well the implementation is going and to be aware of issues as they arise.

Commit to RTI

While using data talking points to motivate staff is recommended, success is affected by making RTI a priority and launching it at the right time. Clear the decks and don't take on too many things at once. If your school is in the first year of implementing a new math curriculum, or has four key teachers serving on curriculum mapping committees, delay the launch date for RTI implementation. October of the first year of implementation is a tough month. As a matter of fact, our client managers always plan the second principals' meeting in November to allow principals to discuss the stress level of their staffs; often principals will contemplate postponing progress monitoring to take some burden off the teachers. However, this is exactly the wrong way to lighten the teachers' load—you'll lose the very data that motivates teachers to keep going because progress monitoring documents the improvements that students are making.

BUILD BUY-IN

In the Illinois district mentioned earlier, principals and district staff referenced that CBM data more than two years later. When they joined me on a webinar to share their experience in implementing RTI, they talked about the defining moment when they collected this baseline data. Uncovering some aspect about your baseline data that will be quoted and remembered years later is helpful. It's got to be simple to be memorable (see Figure 2.4).

Figure 2.4 Build Buy-In

- Attend at least one grade-level team meeting to dialogue about RTI and answer questions
- Meet individually with teachers who may be reluctant or resistant
- Commit to provide support for teachers (release time for planning, budget for needed materials, etc.)
- Celebrate incremental improvements

Handle Reluctance or Resistance

In principals' meetings, one of the most common topics principals bring up is how to handle teachers who are not joining in the implementation. When this topic comes up, begin by categorizing "non-implementers" into two categories, according to the following descriptions:

- *Reluctant:* The reluctant teacher is holding back from fully implementing, yet she is not being vocal about it. Typical reluctant behavior includes doubting whether this is going to work, or whether it will be worth the extra effort, and simply going on as before. Sometimes reluctant teachers are those who are retiring in a year; although, this is not intended as a blanket statement that all retiring teachers resist change. Acknowledge that you understand that they don't want to put the effort into it given they are retiring at year-end. Avoid giving them groups that are the furthest behind. Assign a retiring reluctant teacher a skill that requires the least preparation. It's harder when the reluctant teachers aren't about to retire because, while you can give them a little extra time to see that this is good for students, teachers cannot refuse to implement forever. Once middle-of-year data is available, share the evidence that differentiated instruction has been effective for students and ask the reluctant teacher to get on board and fully implement. Ignoring the refusal to implement usually does not work.

- *Resistant:* The resistant teacher is adamant about not doing it and shares her viewpoint with whomever will listen, potentially undermining the school's implementation. Resisters tend to be driven either by philosophical reasons or by a general dislike of change. The philosophical resister may, for example, have whole-language beliefs about reading instruction and be uncomfortable with systematic and explicit instruction, most likely in phonics. What is difficult is that many times the person who objects is a dedicated teacher whose students do read well. While this teacher has the skills to reach students, some colleagues may not be equally talented, and the open opposition persuades them that noncompliance will be acceptable. In many cases, we've observed that this one resistant teacher has great influence over other teachers at the same grade level, which can poison the implementation from the start.

Why do some teachers resist RTI? In all organizations, people resist change. Expect to have some resistance and plan to deal with it head-on when it happens. Don't let it go underground or continue. Decide how to deal with each person depending on the individual issue. In a district in which there are 10 elementary schools, several principals at a principals' meeting reported that sometimes teachers who resist are frightened of the process. Although there was agreement among the principals that fear is sometimes the motivator, the overwhelming number one issue they discussed was the retiring teacher.

How can a school handle teacher resistance? Much of the responsibility for dealing with resisters falls on the principal; however, there are also some key things that reading coaches, teacher leaders, and fellow teachers (colleagues and team members) can do to keep resisters from derailing the implementation. In most cases, success defeats resistance. Teachers come around when the data shows evidence that this is good for kids and when it's clear that data-differentiated practices are here to stay. Until you have the data, the dialogue can too easily be about philosophy of teaching reading. Once the data is clear that students' scores are improving, then it's not about philosophy. It's about doing what works.

Creating visible data walls is like inoculating to avoid teacher resistance. Data walls provide a shared view for everyone to see what's working, as well as where the building's challenges are. Some schools make diagrams with the three-tier reading pyramid for each grade level and track progress by updating the pyramid throughout the year. They graph the percentage of students at the beginning of the year whose instructional recommendation level is benchmark (green), strategic (yellow), or intensive (red) and track improvements throughout the year. The data walls are updated either three times a year (BOY, MOY, and EOY)[1] or more frequently using periodic progress-monitoring data. As the percentage of students reaching benchmark (green) grows and the percentage that are intensive (red) declines, the evidence that all this extra work is benefitting students is on the wall for everyone to view. Sometimes the data is shown in total for the grade level, and other times all student-data points are plotted within the categories. Some schools use student-identification numbers to keep data confidential and post the data wall in the front office conference room. Other schools place the data wall in a teacher's room where parents cannot view it, and they write student names on sticky notes. One of the best things about data walls is that they reinforce a culture of loyalty to the data. The quickest way to get over philosophical debates about reading instruction is to simply say that you'll use whatever instruction works and the decision criteria for what works is the data.

Creating visible data walls is like inoculating to avoid teacher resistance.

One way to support administrators is to provide a forum for sharing what works. In one district, we facilitated a year-end principals' meeting in June during which each principal and reading coach sat together and filled out a sheet to analyze their year-end CBM data. After they had finished, we asked for a show of hands if the building had above 90% of students at benchmark; one team raised their hands. Then we asked for a show of hands of all schools that had 80% of students above benchmark; three more teams raised their hands. We asked each of these four teams to share what they were doing because it was working.

One of the principals whose students improved shared tips on managing staff resistance. Over the summer, he called in teachers to meet with him in groups or individually. For those who had resisted during the first year, he planned a one-on-one meeting and listened to their reservations. He assured them that this is the direction in which the building is heading, and he offered extra support to them. He arranged a substitute teacher so they could visit a teacher in one of the high-performing schools.

Grade-level teams and reading coaches play a role in neutralizing resistant teachers. The delivery model a grade-level team uses affects

[1]BOY = beginning of year; MOY = middle of year; EOY = end of year.

how easy it is for resisters to continue. If intervention planning and delivery occur within the confines of a teacher's own classroom, then it's possible for a resister to deny students access to effective targeted intervention. However, if the grade-level team is using the walk-to-intervention model, there is pressure (and stress) when one teacher isn't buying in. Oftentimes, the other teachers will express concern privately about letting their students be placed in Miss X's group. The other grade-level teachers understand the value of focused intervention instruction and won't tolerate their colleague's noncompliance. A common solution is that Miss X is assigned a skill where materials can equalize the teacher's effect, such as a computer-based fluency program.

At a different district, when the topic of handling resistant teachers came up, a principal in the room said that she turns up the heat by observing resisters more often. She described how she takes a lesson plan along on an observation and then follows up with a meeting where she asks the teacher to explain why she didn't see sections of the lesson taught. "Can you explain to me why that was missing?" she'll ask. She tells the teacher that she will be back in a couple of weeks to observe again. This principal explained her strategy as follows:

> Let's face it. Teachers don't want the principal in their room that much. I keep going back to observe until she teaches the lesson correctly while I'm there at least. Until they teach the lessons they are supposed to teach, I'll keep coming in and we'll keep talking about it. My strategy is to make it uncomfortable for the noncomplying teacher.

What about the teacher who still doesn't implement RTI after the gift of time, the evidence of data, and the extra coaching and attention? Principals need to engage in difficult conversations with these resistant teachers.

As with any difficult conversation, remember to listen first. Acknowledge that you've observed that the teacher is having difficulty embracing this change. Ask why the instructor objects to it. Probe for objections to surface any fears about insufficient knowledge or skills to do it. Then affirm your commitment to RTI: You've seen how it worked at the district's pilot school or neighboring district, and because your school's data needs to improve, you believe it's right for your students. Explain that as long as you're the principal of this building, it's here to stay. It's not a one-year initiative that will fade away, but the processes associated with small-group, data-differentiated instruction will be sustained. Don't position it as a fad because all teachers know that, in schools, things come and go. Too often, teachers have felt that "this too shall pass." Communicate that this is different. Differentiation is good teaching practice. This is nonnegotiable because it's good for kids.

Now comes the tricky part. Too often, principals stop before this next step. Emphasize that you need the teacher to support and embrace these practices. Then say, "Can I count on you to fully implement and embrace RTI?" (The hardest thing in the world is to not say anything until after the teacher responds.) It's too easy to have the chat and let the educator leave without being put on the spot. Asking this question is critical because it requires a direct answer: *yes, no,* or *maybe.* By getting an answer, the principal is now in a position to remind the teacher of this commitment in a later conversation. In the end, the principal has no choice but to move a teacher who doesn't fully implement RTI to a grade level where resistance will do the least damage and to simultaneously encourage the educator to seek a position at another school.

Provide Support for Teachers

What teachers need the most is extra time for collaboration and planning. In our experience, it's usually not that teachers don't want to do the extra work involved in the assessment and lesson planning. Most teachers are not putting up road blocks; they really *do* need extra time to implement the new practices and processes associated with RTI. Probably the biggest thing you can do to support teachers, even more than buying materials, is to provide extra classroom release time. Teachers probably have the materials, but they need time to get organized and talk to colleagues for help in figuring out what to do.

> Probably the biggest thing you can do to support teachers, even more than buying materials, is to provide extra classroom release time.

A couple of years ago, I invited a principal to copresent a session at a conference. Together we created a joint slide presentation to use during our breakout session, and she added a list of five "whys and hows" for principals, as shown in Figure 2.5.

Figure 2.5 The Five WHYS and HOWS for Principals

Five WHYS for Principals

1. *For Students:* Students who achieve successfully have fewer discipline problems.
2. *For Teachers:* Teachers engaged in meaningful professional development demonstrate more job satisfaction.
3. *For Teams:* Teams become more cohesive as walk-to-intervention planning requires whole grade-level coordination and communication.
4. *For the School:* Investment in early intervention improves learning gains and reduces retentions.
5. *For Administrators:* Proactive leadership is more effective than reactive leadership. Walk-to intervention is an opportunity to "get a step ahead of the game."

(Continued)

Figure 2.5 (Continued)

Five HOWS for Principals

1. *As an Enthusiastic Coach and Cheerleader:* Promote the intervention-group process and express appreciation for staff contributions at faculty meetings, in staff and parent newsletters, and so on.
2. *As a Savvy Budget Manager:* Find a variety of resources for intervention activities, provide a system of check-in and -out for intervention materials, and seek grant support.
3. *As an Accessible Instructional Leader:* Be visible during intervention group walk-throughs, and substitute for a group when time permits for hands-on involvement.
4. *As an Astute Information Manager:* Use data from *DIBELS,* screeners, and progress monitoring for effective decision making.
5. *As a Collaborative Human Resources Developer:* Create a culture of adult learning, support professional development training and arrangements for substitutes, and build commitment to school learning goals and student achievement.

Source: T. Erwin (2007), Geneva Elementary School.

Celebrate Incremental Improvements

Nothing is more important than praise when implementing RTI, because you're asking teachers to put in extra effort to learn something new. Therefore, plan celebrations throughout the year and don't wait until year-end. Celebrating successes along the way helps boost buy-in of the reluctant teachers who are holding back, and it solidifies the commitment of the early adopters. Celebrations come in all forms, including private and public.

Private celebrations are when principals or reading coaches put a note in a teacher's box or say something about a small-group's improvement in their scores. Grade-level colleagues can also observe these improvements if the entire team has access to the scores. A comment from one teacher to another makes a difference, such as noticing how many students in a colleague's group made significant gains, or how well the student from the teacher's own class is doing with the skill instruction received in another's intervention group.

The most common public celebration is when the principal attends a grade-level team meeting to express thanks for the gains. For example, when the reports show that the number of students at benchmark grew from 38% to 57% between September and January, a visit from the principal and an acknowledgment of the success is well deserved. But there are many other ways to publicly acknowledge both teams and individual teachers: Ask four staff members to stand up because they each contributed to a child's success in reaching benchmark; plan a pizza party for the team that reaches its middle-of-year goal; invite a district staff member to come to an afterschool faculty meeting to recognize the data improvements.

CREATE THE RTI TEAM

Creating the RTI team in each school is an important step to complete during the planning stage (see Figure 2.6). In this section, we'll explore why this is important, as well as what the role of the team will be, so that you can place the right people on the team. The two major reasons to form a team are to build buy-in and to get help in completing tasks. Seeking input is part of creating a team. If you want others to come along, it's a good idea to involve them and seek their input from the start and throughout the process.

Figure 2.6 Create the RTI Team

- **Create a School RTI Team**
  - Assistant principal, reading coach, Title I coordinator, special education coordinator, grade-level team representatives, school psychologist, speech-language pathologist
- **Appoint an RTI Coordinator**
  - Evaluate skills of possible candidates compared to job description
  - Name an RTI coordinator
  - Define the position
  - Inform staff of the role of the RTI coordinator

At an RTI conference, I heard another presenter relate something that happened while she was working in her organization's booth at a reading conference. When a principal walked into the booth, the presenter began with the conversation starter, "Are you doing RTI?" The principal responded, "Yes, but it's a lot of work, so I'm doing it without involving my teachers." There's a fundamental misconception here. There's no way to "do RTI" without the teachers analyzing student data, participating in group placement decisions, and teaching the small groups.

Create a School RTI Team

One of the most exciting opportunities when implementing RTI is exactly that: getting all the teachers involved. RTI represents one of the most significant opportunities for a school to align all staff members under one umbrella to make decisions about students based on data. I've seen silos break down between special and general education and between ELL and general education, as well as between Title I and unfunded schools. As mentioned previously in this book, it's amazing how many times I've heard principals say that one of the best things about having implemented RTI is that teachers at a grade level now say "our kids."

Who should be on the school RTI team? Appointing the right staff members to serve on a school's RTI team is critical. Construct your team to include all opinion leaders. Recommended team members follow:

- Assistant principal
- Reading coach or reading teacher (the content experts)
- Title I coordinator
- Special education coordinator
- Grade-level team representatives
- School psychologist
- Speech-language pathologist

What is the role of the school-based RTI team? One of the team's key roles is to develop RTI processes in the school. The team provides advice and helps administrators make decisions to put processes in place so that teachers can do their work. When developing processes, the following questions should be addressed:

- Who will administer the assessments?
- How do we analyze the data once we have it?
- How do we place students in groups?
- What training and support do teachers need to be successful?
- What will our problem-solving procedure look like? How will we decide when it's time to refer a student for testing for special education?
- What do we do when a student is not making progress? What can we offer students when instruction is not working?

This team takes the pulse of the implementation in the building. When team members meet, they discuss which grade levels are implementing smoothly and where it's not going well. They talk about where there is confusion and what needs to be clarified to address staff questions and issues. A principal cannot do it alone; that is why the team is so important.

Appoint an RTI Coordinator

Most buildings have a designated point person for RTI. Responsibilities for RTI coordinators can align with one of two options:

- Option 1: Responsibilities are mainly in the area of assessment.
- Option 2: Responsibilities include assessment plus peer coaching on instruction.

The logical candidate for the RTI coordinator depends on which view of the coordinator's position your school adopts.

What is the role of the RTI coordinator? Our recommendation for the role of the RTI coordinator is outlined in the job description in Table 2.2.

Table 2.2 Job Description of RTI Coordinator

<table>
<tr><td>Prerequisite Skills</td><td>• Possesses a strong understanding of reading development and effective instructional practices to teach reading to struggling readers
• Collaborates well with teachers
• Enjoys working with data</td></tr>
<tr><td>Primary Responsibilities</td><td>• Administration of assessments
o Oversees the assessment calendar
o Orders assessment materials
o Organizes storage system for student scoring booklets
o Manages the assessment team (if there is one)
o Organizes schedule for rotating substitutes during assessment periods
o Trains teachers in how to administer assessments
o Provides review sessions on critical administration rules and procedures before each benchmark period
• Data collection and reporting
o Coordinates collection of data from assessment teams and classroom teachers
o Distributes reports to teachers
o Coordinates distributing data to educators for special education, Title I, speech-language pathology, and English as a second language on students they service
o Prepares and frequently updates principal's data notebook
• Coordination of RTI processes
o Attends grade-level team meeting to coordinate RTI processes across the grade levels
o Serves as liaison between the principal and teachers on the RTI initiative</td></tr>
<tr><td>Additional Responsibilities</td><td>• Data analysis
o Meets with teachers individually or in grade-level teams to help interpret data
o Instructs teachers in data-analysis procedures, including error-pattern analysis of items on student probes
o Helps teachers place students in intervention groups and define focus of instruction for each group
• Planning intervention instruction for each group
o Assists teachers in preparing materials and strategies for each group
• Instructional coaching
o Models effective intervention group instruction for teachers
o Observes teachers instructing intervention groups and provides feedback and coaching</td></tr>
</table>

Source: From Hall (2008), p. 47.

Whether you choose Option 1 or 2, the responsibilities in the area of data analysis are the same. Someone needs to take charge of all the assessment and data processes. Typically, the RTI coordinator ensures that all the assessments are completed on time and administered correctly and that the data is available from the data-management system. This responsibility includes the following tasks:

- Inform entire staff about which assessments are given and dates for completion.
- Teach appropriate staff to administer the assessments and continually train new staff, as needed.
- Instruct staff in how to enter the data into the reporting system and how to print appropriate reports.
- Help staff learn to analyze and interpret the data.
- Show staff how to place students in groups.

In addition to facilitating a smooth and stress-free assessment period, the RTI coordinator typically ensures that there is consistency between grade levels. She attends grade-level meetings, keeps everybody informed, and communicates important messages about the processes so that teams aren't veering off and doing things in a manner that is inconsistent with the rest of the grade levels. The RTI coordinator acts on behalf of the principal in matters related to the implementation because the principal cannot be at all the grade-level meetings. Many principals have a regularly scheduled weekly meeting with their RTI coordinator, who not only updates the data reports in the principal's notebook but also, during meetings, points out the important insights revealed by the data.

If your school chooses to define the RTI coordinator's role more like Option 2, then there are additional responsibilities that relate to supporting the instruction provided in the groups. The role then expands to take on duties that are more like those of the reading coach, with responsibilities for helping teachers make instructional decisions. This includes meeting individually with teachers to not only talk about student data but also plan which instructional materials and strategies will best address the deficit skills. The RTI coordinator may model a lesson, observe the teacher during instruction, and then provide feedback and help set goals. When the school doesn't have the correct materials, the RTI coordinator recommends materials for purchase, orders them, and then trains teachers to use them. This colleague-mentoring role works only if there is a relationship of trust. Teachers are typically more open if there is someone in the building they can trust to ask questions, brainstorm with, and access as a resource.

In one school we observed last year, 64 out of 86 first-grade students needed interventions in phonological awareness at the beginning of the year. The 30 minutes of differentiation time in kindergarten had not been used well. Unfortunately, there is a cascading effect between grade levels because if kindergarten intervention instruction is weak, it affects Grade 1 and so on. When Option 2 is chosen, the RTI coordinator needs to be available to walk through and observe groups during intervention time. Therefore, the RTI coordinator will not have time to teach small groups as a reading specialist all day and walk through and observe as well. Some schools appoint their reading specialist as the RTI coordinator and then free up time by reducing the number of groups the specialist teaches daily. In addition, the RTI coordinator is often relieved of teaching groups on key days to attend grade-level meetings. This person needs "office hours" to be available when teachers have planning and collaboration time, so they can stop by and talk about a group or student.

If your building has a full-time reading coach already, then the reading coach is most likely your RTI coordinator. Schools that do not have full-time reading coaches will need to appoint a person to facilitate and oversee the implementation of RTI.

In one district where there were reading coaches in only the 5 Reading First buildings of the 10 elementary schools, we advised our district contact that it would be incredibly helpful in this implementation if there was one person in every building who was designated as the day-to-day contact. If you use an outside consultant, it's critical to identify key staff and make sure that the consultant is focused on building local capacity of these key staff members.

Typically, the RTI coordinator is more likely to be a reading specialist than a full-time classroom teacher because the coordinator's time needs to be flexible. Conversely, if Option1 is chosen, then there are many more people who could serve as the RTI coordinator, including the school psychologist or speech-language pathologist (SLP). (In some schools, the SLPs or special education teachers work for a multidistrict cooperative, so this may not be possible.) Professional development can be more narrowly focused on assessment administration and data analysis.

Districts that choose to use Option 2 for the RTI coordinator will need to provide more training for these staff members. The RTI coordinator will need professional development focused not only on assessment administration and data analysis but also on instructional strategies and peer coaching. If implementing districtwide, plan RTI coordinators' meetings to collaborate, share, and avoid reinventing the wheel in multiple schools.

What authority does the RTI coordinator have? RTI coordinators, like reading coaches, can be successful only when other staff members respect and trust them; the principal is the person who gives the RTI coordinator authority. The RTI coordinator has no authority over any staff members. However, it's absolutely necessary for the principal to give the RTI coordinator authority related to the tasks of the role—authority to require that all the other staff members submit their data on time and authority to monitor the assessment process—not only to keep on schedule but also to ensure assessment fidelity so the data will be useful.

PLANNING PERIOD

Getting ready for implementation requires a planning period to motivate staff, build buy-in, and create a team, as described in this chapter (see Table 2.3).

Table 2.3 Planning Period Before Launching RTI (March to August)

Time Period	Assessment	Data Analysis and Grouping	Instruction	Problem-Solving Process
March	Select CBM assessment instrument. Train assessment team to administer and score CBM, and enter data into data-management system.		Begin presentations to grade-level teams about the principles and terms or language of RTI.	Appoint RTI data team members. Begin meeting weekly.
			Add 30- to 40-minute intervention blocks in master schedule for next year.	
			Identify additional support staff (aides, etc.) who can teach groups next year.	

Time Period	Assessment	Data Analysis and Grouping	Instruction	Problem-Solving Process
April	Practice administering alternate form of CBM to limited group of students (assessment team administers the CBM).			Appoint RTI coordinator. Announce responsibilities and role to all staff.
	Select diagnostic screeners for phonological awareness and phonics. Train assessment team in administration, scoring, and data-entry procedures of diagnostic assessments.		Make inventory of programs and materials for intervention instruction.	Review state guidelines for special education eligibility criteria (data team).
May	Train grade-level team leaders on administration guidelines of assessment.		Order any initial materials needed.	Discuss use of data walls. Discuss use of data boards for each grade level for regrouping.
	Administer baseline CBM to all students.	Analyze baseline CBM data (RTI team). Create pyramid chart for each grade level. Determine three to four *data talking points* for school. Develop plan to address any weaknesses in Tier I core instruction.	Discuss baseline-data results: Develop motivation for *why* school is implementing RTI.	
			Determine service delivery model for how groups will be taught at each grade level.	

(Continued)

Table 2.3 (Continued)

Time Period	Assessment	Data Analysis and Grouping	Instruction	Problem-Solving Process
June and July			Organize intervention materials in a library. Develop check-out system.	
			Provide summer training for instructional aides who will teach intervention groups.	
			Consider instructional space needs for intervention groups.	

CONCLUSION

This chapter discussed the key initial steps of getting ready to implement an RTI plan at the school level. "Getting ready" is the planning process where an overarching goal is to build buy-in among school staff. We discussed using baseline data to generate two to three data talking points as a "call to action" for staff. It's also important not to skip other steps that can lead to buy-in, or jeopardize RTI from the start. Appointing an RTI team and someone to coordinate the effort accomplishes many objectives and is completed during the getting ready stage.

Additional materials and resources related to *Jumpstart RTI: Using RTI in Your Elementary School Right Now* can be found at http://my.95percentgroup.com/Jumpstart.

3

Getting Started

Once your school has assembled an RTI team and has appointed an RTI coordinator, follow this set of tasks as you launch into implementation (see Figure 3.1). The following steps should be completed during the "getting started" stage before intervention groups meet. First, create an assessment plan (see Figure 3.2).

CREATE AN ASSESSMENT PLAN

To implement RTI, a school will need to have appropriate assessments and a schedule for when each assessment is delivered. Some initial steps follow:

1. Use curriculum-based measures.
   - Select assessment instruments.
     - Select one curriculum-based measure (e.g., *DIBELS* or *AIMSweb*) as a universal screener.
   - Train staff in the administration of the CBM.
   - Complete the baseline assessment.
     - Quantify school need for RTI.
     - Use data to identify two or three data talking points.
2. Use informal diagnostic screeners.
   - Select diagnostic assessments for phonological awareness and phonics (e.g., *PASI* and *PSI*) to measure skill mastery for students identified as at risk on CBM.
   - Train staff in the administration of the diagnostic screeners.
     - Begin with an assessment team, and then train teachers (if you do it for them, they will never completely "own" the data).

3. Publish a calendar of benchmark and progress-monitoring dates.
   - Include three benchmarks.
   - Include at least eight progress-monitoring periods per year.

Figure 3.1 Structures

Structures

Create an Assessment Plan	Select a Delivery Model	Add Intervention Blocks to the School Master Schedule
• **CBM** • Select curriculum-based measurement (CBM) assessment instrument • Train at least an assessment team • Administer baseline CBM • Develop data talking points from the baseline • **Informal Diagnostic Screeners** • Research and select phonological awareness, phonics, and comprehension assessments • Train staff • **Assessment Calendar** • Publish a calendar of benchmark and progress-monitoring dates	• List alternate models: in-classroom vs. walk-to intervention • Meet to evaluate models, and select one for each grade level • Brainstom a list of all other staff to teach intervention groups	• Determine the amount of time for intervention by grade level (30, 40, or 45 minutes) • Add intervention blocks for each grade level staggered throughout the day • Determine which staff can “flood” each grade level to help teach intervention groups

Figure 3.2 Create an Assessment Plan

- **CBM**
  - Select curriculum-based measurement (CBM) assessment instrument
  - Train at least an assessment team
  - Administer baseline CBM
  - Develop data talking points from the baseline
- **Informal Diagnostic Screeners**
  - Research and select phonological awareness, phonics, and comprehension assessments
  - Train staff
- **Assessment Calendar**
  - Publish a calendar of benchmark and progress-monitoring dates

When selecting assessment instruments, many schools are missing one important factor: diagnostic assessments. Trying to use a CBM for everything is a serious flaw at the outset of implementation. CBMs are perfect for universal screening and to identify students who have deficits. Yet, that's just step one—more assessment is needed.

The medical-model analogy is helpful here. When you go to the doctor or emergency room, a nurse determines how urgently you need attention based on your vital signs. Doctors don't base their diagnosis solely on the three vital signs; additional information from the patient can point to more diagnostic testing. CBM data is a great "urgency indicator," and it even directs the teacher toward determining which diagnostic assessment to administer next. If a kindergarten student scores below 10 on the first sound fluency (FSF) indicator on the beginning-of-year *DIBELS Next* assessment, the teacher's next step is to figure out what the student does know. Does the student segment and blend syllables and onset-rimes but struggle at the phoneme level? If a third-grade student's median oral reading fluency (ORF) score of the three passages is 20 points below the benchmark of 110, the teacher's next step is to determine whether it's an accuracy or fluency issue. Once the teacher discovers that the student's accuracy rate is below 95% on all three passages, he knows to administer a phonics screener to pinpoint the word patterns the student is missing. Trying to group from CBM data is perhaps the most common mistake schools make while first beginning RTI.

Trying to group from CBM data is perhaps the most common mistake schools make while first beginning RTI.

Another common assessment problem emerges when teachers aren't trained in administering assessments. If you use assessment teams to complete initial screening, we highly recommend moving the responsibility for assessment, data analysis, and grouping from the assessment team to the teachers and the grade-level teams. In schools where the reading coach or assessment team administers all the assessments, the teachers don't buy in because they never understand data to the same extent.

Assessing too often is another common issue. During the first year of implementation, teachers learn to use the data to inform instructional decisions. They need time to learn how to administer and interpret the data too. Some schools insist on progress monitoring students weekly. It's better to start out slower and increase frequency once the data is being fully used. Published assessment calendars help clarify for the entire staff the expected frequency of progress monitoring. Most schools tie regrouping to the assessment calendar. This enables grade-level teams to move students between groups based on "fresh" data.

Published assessment calendars help clarify for the entire staff the expected frequency of progress monitoring. Most schools tie regrouping to the assessment calendar. This enables grade-level teams to move students between groups based on "fresh" data.

The next step is to determine your phase-in approach:

- Decide to implement in a limited number of grade levels the first year (for example, kindergarten and Grade 1).
- Start with the building's lowest grade levels and work up.

Consider the following example before deciding to implement in kindergarten through Grade 5 all at once. A district decided to implement a pilot (which we highly recommend) to get RTI practices and processes in place at only kindergarten and Grade 1 in three of ten elementary schools. In the spring of the first year, the board approved lengthening the elementary school day by 30 minutes and mandated that this time be used to provide an intervention or differentiation block for kindergarten through Grade 5 at all buildings. However, there was only funding to support yearlong professional development for the kindergarten through Grade 1 teachers at all buildings; teachers for Grades 2 through 5 got only one workshop, some assessments, and no follow-up support.

Principals at every meeting talked about the stress level of the Grade 2 through 5 teachers, who perceived that they were on their own to figure out how to interpret the data, place students in small groups, and plan curriculum for intervention. One of the principals pointed out that the upper elementary teachers didn't have the training or language about reading instruction that the lower grade teachers did. Another principal shared that her Grade 3 teachers had given the CBM and the phonics diagnostic assessments where necessary. They could see all the students' deficits but realized that they didn't have the skills to deliver effective intervention instruction.

The concern is twofold: (1) When teachers don't get support, there is a risk that the practices they put in place will be misguided, and (2) if the upper grade teachers are disgruntled, it may spoil the enthusiasm of the lower grade teachers and upset the building's entire implementation.

It is far better to implement at kindergarten through Grade 1 the first year and do it really well. Implementing RTI well at kindergarten through Grade 1 builds a firewall to stop students moving into Grades 2 and above with deficits. Research recommends early intervention because it takes fewer intervention minutes to get results. The National Institute of Child Health and Human Development (NICHD) branch of the National Institutes of Health shows evidence that it takes four times as long to improve a student's skills in Grade 4 as it does in kindergarten; that means that it would take two hours of intervention in fourth grade to provide the same improvement as 30 minutes in kindergarten.

Implementing RTI well at kindergarten through Grade 1 builds a firewall to stop students moving into Grades 2 and above with deficits.

Keep in mind that it takes about a year to help teachers learn all the new processes and instructional strategies and get comfortable with them. In one district, the administrators told the staff up front the following message:

> We will be implementing at all grade levels eventually. We have a job to do at kindergarten and Grade 1, and it will take about a year. We will move to Grade 2 as soon as kindergarten and Grade 1 are solid. Then we'll move up the other grades more quickly.

Concentrating on just two grade levels initially should minimize the teachers' stress level as they are learning new practices. In addition, the data at kindergarten and Grade 1 shows progress quickly, which motivates the other grade levels to implement. The data will not show the improvements as quickly at the other grade levels because there are more skills that can be lagging and the gap is wider. It's important to realize that it may take several years for the improvements in the CBM data to be evident in the third-grade state assessments.

> It's important to realize that it may take several years for the improvements in the CBM data to be evident in the third-grade state assessments.

Districts that have been implementing RTI practices at the elementary level for several years begin to look ahead at what they will do at middle and high schools. While many of the same assessments and processes are effective, there are some key differences. Scheduling is more challenging at middle and senior high school, and addressing the knowledge base is also tricky. Teachers at these levels generally have not been trained in reading development or how to teach reading and often don't view it as their job. Our experience is that it's best to select a few teachers who will provide intervention and train them to teach particular skill areas. Some teach phonics groups, others take the fluency groups, and still others teach the comprehension groups.

Establish RTI Structures

The structural decisions (the decisions that create the design of the assessment plan, the delivery model, and the intervention blocks) set in place the framework that teachers need to be able to teach the groups. Most of these structural decisions are made by the administrators, either at the district level or within a building. These decisions, when combined, determine the number of minutes of intervention students will receive, which in turn shapes not only the building's assessment calendar but also the school's master schedule. Therefore, it's helpful to see the connection between the individual decisions.

While trying to take RTI to scale across an entire district, it becomes evident that each of these decisions impacts the number of intervention minutes. If a grade-level team quickly finishes their data analysis and the students are all placed in groups a week after the CBM window closes, this grade level will deliver 2½ hours more of intervention time (per student) per week compared to a team who takes more time to figure it out. The start date of the groups is thus important. Within a particular district, the start dates varied from September 21 to October 12. In addition, some schools did not have intervention on early release day, so they were using a four-day versus five-day intervention schedule. To make the point, at a November principals' meeting, we showed a chart of cumulative hours (Table 3.1) of intervention instruction from the start of school through November 10 for these two schedules.

Table 3.1 Cumulative Hours of Four-Day Versus Five-Day Intervention Schedules From Various Start Dates Through November 10

Start Date	Four-Day Intervention	Five-Day Intervention
September 21	15 hours	18.5 hours
October 12	10 hours	13.5 hours

Notice that when a team provided intervention four days a week starting October 12, students had received only 10 hours of intervention by November 10. Compare this with a team that started three weeks earlier and used a five-day-a-week model: These students had received nearly twice the number of hours of intervention (18.5 vs. 10 hours).

An additional variable that affects intensity of intervention is related to the size of the groups. Pulling all available staff to "flood" the grade level reduces the size of some of the groups. In smaller groups, instructors can provide more corrective feedback and practice cycles. A principal recently asked whether it was better to have some students working independently to free up a teacher to make intervention groups smaller. The answer is yes; it's better to have benchmark students meaningfully engaged in reading and writing about text so that a teacher can be freed up to take a group if groups are too large.

Pulling all available staff to "flood" the grade level reduces the size of some of the groups. In smaller groups, instructors can provide more corrective feedback and practice cycles.

In addition, materials can impact the intensity of instruction. When teachers use more activities and less explicit instruction, the impact is less than it could be and students won't make progress as quickly.

Find the Time for Intervention

When you suggest that a teacher needs to add 30 minutes of intervention, the reaction is always predictable: How can I fit intervention into an already crowded day? Because teachers don't feel that there's enough time to do everything they are already asked to do, it is critical to tackle the time issue up front. Administrators need to take responsibility for this and take the burden of trying to decide when to fit intervention into the schedule. For that reason, we recommend revising the school master schedule to add a 30-minute intervention block outside of the regular reading block for all implementation grades. Intervention should add minutes of instruction in reading rather than taking from the core instruction. Staggering the blocks across the day enables using an all-hands-on-deck approach of flooding a grade level with support staff. If more than one grade level has the same intervention time, it will be impossible to have enough staff members to make group sizes small. Administrators need to decide what else won't be done to make time for interventions. Quite often, the schedule is adjusted to squeeze out enough time for the intervention blocks. Often science and social science are integrated into the intervention time by adding in text on those topics.

Intervention should add minutes of instruction in reading rather than taking from the core instruction.

We recommend daily intervention. Not only will students accumulate intervention minutes more quickly, but when groups meet only three times a week, too much focus is lost between lessons and more time is spent in reviewing than when intervention occurs daily. Except for beginning kindergarten students, 30 minutes is ideal because when the length is shorter, the time goes by too quickly once the group settles down. However, sometimes kindergarten groups meet for a shorter period the first half of the year.

Group size is also critical. Maintain the smallest groups for those furthest behind and larger groups for fluency, comprehension, and enrichment.

Group size is also critical. Maintain the smallest groups for those furthest behind and larger groups for fluency, comprehension, and enrichment.

SELECT A DELIVERY MODEL

The *delivery model* is the organizational approach to delivering the small-group instruction—who teaches which small groups in what location (see Figure 3.3).

The RTI coordinator and principal facilitate discussions so that each grade-level team can select a delivery model. Each grade-level team needs to decide which model to use so that they believe in it, work for it,

Figure 3.3 Select a Delivery Model

- List alternate models: in-classroom vs. walk-to intervention
- Meet to evaluate models, and select one for each grade level
- Brainstom a list of all other staff to teach intervention groups

and support it. This level of commitment is most likely to happen when teachers have a voice in selecting the approach their grade-level team uses. Two common approaches are (1) students stay in their own classroom and receive instruction there, or (2) students walk to the location where their group is meeting (walk-to intervention). When students stay in their own classroom for intervention, an assistant or reading specialist "pushes in" to teach one skill, the classroom teacher teaches another intervention group, and the benchmark students work at literacy workstations in the classroom.

The walk-to-intervention approach, where students are grouped across a grade level, has very different implications. Students from each classroom are placed in skill groups based on what the data shows as their deficit skill. Imagine a third-grade team of four teachers and three other staff members. Table 3.2 shows the placement of students across the seven groups during the 30-minute differentiation block.

Table 3.2 Student Placement in Seven Groups During 30-Minute Intervention Block

Skill Group	Number of Students	Teacher	Location
Enrichment or acceleration (benchmark)	28	Media specialist	Library
Comprehension	22	Classroom teacher 1	Classroom 1
Fluency	22	Instructional aide	Computer lab
Multisyllable words	8	Classroom teacher 2	Classroom 2
Vowel teams	6	Classroom teacher 3	Classroom 3
Long vowel silent-*e*	4	Classroom teacher 4	Classroom 4
Consonant-vowel-consonant (CVC)	4	Reading specialist	Reading specialist's room
Total (7 groups)	**94**	**7 staff members**	

At the beginning of the year with the walk-to-intervention approach (Figure 3.4), teachers assign students to groups after finishing assessing them on the CBM and diagnostic screeners. Teachers must agree to variable-sized groups, with some staff having larger groups for the benchmark and nearly benchmark skill groups while other staff members have smaller groups of students who are furthest behind. In addition, other staff members may be considered for teaching intervention groups in either of the models described previously.

Figure 3.4 Walk-to-Intervention Approach

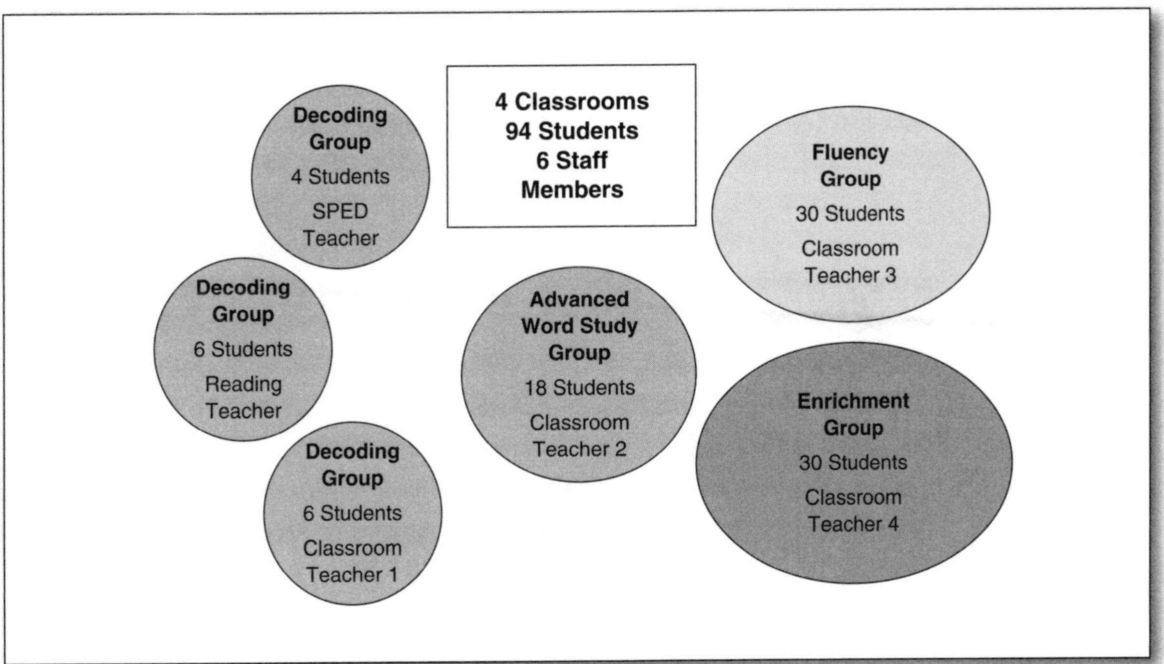

While it's possible to do the push-in approach without collaborating with peers, the walk-to-intervention model requires team cooperation. In fact, with the walk-to-intervention approach, one of the biggest benefits is that it forces collaboration.

The walk-to-intervention model requires team cooperation. In fact, with the walk-to-intervention approach, one of the biggest benefits is that it forces collaboration.

A principal of a different district spoke at a conference breakout session about the benefits of a fully implemented walk-to-intervention approach in her school:

> The students delight in getting to go to a different teacher for those 30 minutes a day. We now have laser precision in identifying mastered and deficit skills and then grouping appropriately to teach those skills. Now the teachers say "our kids," not "my kids."

One of my second-grade teachers said, "Can I recall the last 25 years of my students? If I could just have them back, I could teach them to read with the skills I now have." It's been an amazing and worthwhile journey.

ADD INTERVENTION BLOCKS

Although difficult to prepare, the master schedule needs to include intervention time; if it is on the schedule, it will be considered a priority and will more likely be done (see Figure 3.5). By adding intervention time to the master schedule, teachers do not need to figure out how to fit it into their already tight schedules. Also, the principal and reading coach can more easily monitor interventions because they will know when they are scheduled (see Figure 3.6).

> Although difficult to prepare, the master schedule needs to include intervention time; if it is on the schedule, it will be considered a priority and will more likely be done.

Figure 3.5 Add Intervention Blocks to the School Master Schedule

- Determine the amount of time for intervention by grade level (30, 40, or 45 minutes)
- Add intervention blocks for each grade level staggered throughout the day
- Determine which staff can "flood" each grade level to help teach intervention groups

Determine Who Teaches Intervention Groups

Each school needs to evaluate and decide which staff members will be dedicated to teaching small groups during the intervention blocks. In order to get group sizes small enough, at least 50% more staff than the number of classroom teachers must flood the grade level. If you have four second-grade classrooms, you'll need at least two additional staff members so there can be six groups. If you have more than 50% of students below benchmark, you'll need even more staff flooding the grade level.

What type of additional staff members teach intervention groups? It depends on the resources and funding in your building, but Title I aides and teachers are scheduled to rotate across grade levels throughout the day to teach intervention groups that are integrated into this approach. An eternal debate is whether it's appropriate to have paraprofessionals teaching the lowest students. While in a perfect world only certified teachers teach every intervention group, that's not realistic. Furthermore, certified teachers aren't always better at instruction than instructional assistants. Some paraprofessionals are superior to classroom teachers at teaching intervention groups. If paraprofessionals teach intervention groups, two things are

Figure 3.6 Master Schedule

Sample School Master Schedule

TIME	KINDERGARTEN	FIRST GRADE	SECOND GRADE	THIRD GRADE	COACH
8:00	Core Reading Block	Homeroom	Homeroom	Homeroom	Prep
8:05					
8:10					
8:15		Core Reading Block	Core Reading Block	In-Class Intervention	Observe Core Reading Block
8:20					
8:25					
8:30					
8:35					
8:40	In-Class Intervention			Core Reading Block	
8:45					
8:50					
8:55					
9:00					
9:05	Core Reading Block				
9:10					
9:15					
9:20					
9:25					
9:30					
9:35		Spelling	In-Class Intervention		
9:40	Recess				
9:45				Recess	
9:50					Prep
9:55	Instructional Time				
10:00		Recess	Recess	Block 1	
10:05					
10:10				1 Math; 2 Science and Social Science Benchmark and Intervention Groups	
10:15		In-Class Intervention	Music, Arts, and Crafts		First Grade Intervention
10:20					
10:25					
10:30		Math	Planning Time and Specials		
10:35					
10:40					Third Grade and Second Grade Intervention
10:45					
10:50					
10:55					
11:00					
11:05					
11:10					
11:15				Lunch	
11:20			Lunch		
11:25					
11:30		Music, Arts, and Crafts			
11:35				Block 2	
11:40			Science and Social Science Pull-Out Intervention		
11:45		Lunch		1 Science and Social Science Benchmark and Intervention Groups; 2 Math	
11:50					
11:55	Lunch				
12:00					
12:05		Planning Time and Specials			
12:10					
12:15					
12:20	Instructional Time				
12:25					Lunch
12:30					
12:35					
12:40			Language Arts and Spelling		
12:45					
12:50		Language Arts			
12:55	Pull-Out Intervention			In-Class Intervention	Kindergarten Intervention
1:00					
1:05					
1:10					
1:15					
1:20					
1:25					
1:30	Instructional Time	Recess	Recess	Recess	Prep
1:35					
1:40					
1:45	Recess	Science and Social Science Pull-Out Intervention	Math	Planning Time and Specials	First Grade Intervention
1:50					
1:55					
2:00	Instructional Time				
2:05					
2:10					
2:15					Third Grade Intervention
2:20					
2:25					
2:30					
2:35					
2:40		Language Arts			
2:45					
2:50					
2:55					

Source: Provided by 95 Percent Group Inc. (2007d).

Some paraprofessionals are superior to classroom teachers at teaching intervention groups. If paraprofessionals teach intervention groups, two things are important: They need to be trained, and they need to be supervised.

important: They need to be trained, and they need to be supervised. If you are concerned about a paraprofessional's skills, assign groups where there are excellent materials with lessons that are more scripted. When it comes to enlisting the help of paraprofessionals in teaching intervention groups, make decisions on a case-by-case basis. Generalities don't work here.

One school in Kansas that we advised nearly 10 years ago invested several years into implementation of what is now called RTI. Each time one of our consultants provided professional development (PD), she noticed that the paraprofessionals were more involved in the PD than the classroom teachers. The school's approach was to leave the benchmark students in the classroom while the paraprofessionals pull out selected students and provide all the differentiated instruction. Their scores rose across several years; however, I learned a number of years later that once the building lost its Title I funding because of the high reading scores, the teachers were unable to carry on because they hadn't invested in learning the process. Our advice to all schools is that the classroom teachers and other support staff need to fully collaborate; classroom teachers need to be teaching some of the lowest groups.

Decide What Is Taught During Intervention Time

Intervention time is sacred. This is a unique opportunity to meet students' needs in groups that are focused and targeted. It's just as beneficial for an above-benchmark student to be in a literacy circle discussing above-level text with peers as it is for a struggling student to be in a group of four students getting instant correction and repetition in order to master recognizing words with a long vowel silent-*e* pattern. As one district administrator said, "With the walk-to model, we are giving instructional specificity to lower students and giving the acceleration groups the gift of time." However, too often when schools implement, they don't pay enough attention to what is taught during intervention time. Each group teacher must provide powerful, targeted, and useful instruction that meets the needs of the carefully grouped students in front of him. A lot of time and effort went into assessing, analyzing, diagnosing, and arranging for these 30 minutes of intervention to happen during the school day. If any group is not on task, it's a huge lost opportunity for students.

Intervention time is sacred. This is a unique opportunity to meet students' needs in groups that are focused and targeted.

YEAR 1: FIRST HALF

The steps to get started are shown in Table 3.3, which depicts the steps that need to occur during the first half of the first year.

Table 3.3 Year 1: First Half

Time Period	Assessment	Data Analysis and Grouping	Instruction	Problem-Solving Process
Planning period before school starts*	Train all teachers and support staff to administer CBM and diagnostic assessments.			
First 2 weeks of school	Administer diagnostic screener to students whose previous year spring CBM indicates deficiencies (kindergarten is based on teacher observation).	Place at-risk students in temporary intervention groups.	Identify all staff available to teach intervention groups—consider training needs.	
From second week of school until CBM fall benchmark	Review administration procedures for CBM and diagnostic assessments.		Provide instruction in temporary groups using regular intervention materials.	Meet with data team to begin discussing the problem-solving process (principal).
September CBM fall benchmark (2-week window)	Administer CBM to all students within a two-week time frame, and enter all data in CBM data-management system.	Analyze CBM data to determine which students need diagnostic screeners. Assess with diagnostic screeners (PA or phonics).	Continue teaching temporary intervention groups during the two-week CBM assessment window.	Meet with RTI coordinator to problem-solve any assessment issues (principal).

(Continued)

Table 3.3 (Continued)

Time Period	Assessment	Data Analysis and Grouping	Instruction	Problem-Solving Process
September	Rescreen 10% of students randomly selected with CBM alternate form (assessment team).	Analyze random rescreening against original. Address any issues.		
September—week after fall (BOY) benchmark	Administer diagnostic screeners to all below-benchmark, or inaccurate-benchmark, students (PA or phonics).	Analyze CBM and diagnostic data and place students in initial groups (teachers).		Attend grade-level team meetings to discuss data and agenda of problem-solving meetings (principal).
September and October—second week after fall benchmark		Train teachers on intervention logs.	Begin initial groups.	
October	Administer progress-monitoring assessment (Assessment Number 2 with alternate forms). Use diagnostic or CBM to monitor progress; match assessment to skill-group focus.	Regroup mid- to late October. Move students who are at mastery level on progress monitoring up to group for next deficit skill.	Observe and coach intervention teachers.	After Assessment Number 3, meet to discuss progress rates of all students based on three data points. Evaluate the overall effectiveness of groups (data team).
November	Assess benchmark students once with CBM to avoid surprises.	Regroup at least monthly. Exit students to benchmark if at least two data points are at benchmark level.	Intensify instruction for students not making sufficient progress.	After Assessment Number 4, sign up to bring individual students to problem-solving meeting. Discuss potential referrals for testing for learning disabilities (teachers).

Time Period	Assessment	Data Analysis and Grouping	Instruction	Problem-Solving Process
December	Continue periodic progress-monitoring assessments.	Continue reviewing progress-monitoring data and moving students.		Continue bimonthly or weekly problem-solving meetings; discuss students.
December and January middle (MOY) benchmark	Administer middle-of-year (MOY) CBM benchmark assessment.	Regroup. Identify students whose rate of progress is insufficient.	Evaluate Tier III materials and programs.	

*Refer to Table 2.3, "Planning Period Before Launching RTI," for a breakdown of this before-school planning period.

CONCLUSION

Chapter 3 continued the discussion of RTI implementation at the school level with a focus on the steps to get started. There are several assessment steps to complete, including collecting baseline CBM data and selecting diagnostic assessment instruments. The final tasks to accomplish during the getting-started stage are to make the decisions that establish the structure for RTI: adding intervention blocks to the school's master schedule, selecting a delivery model, and allocating extra staff to "flood" the grade level and help the classroom teachers keep groups small.

Additional materials and resources related to *Jumpstart RTI: Using RTI in Your Elementary School Right Now* can be found at http://my.95percentgroup.com/Jumpstart.

4

Analyzing Data and Forming Groups

In Chapter 1, we explored what RTI looks like when fully implemented, as well as the gains in reading scores achieved by a district that rolled it out across 38 schools over five years. Then Chapters 2 and 3 provided information about planning the structure needed to launch RTI in a school, including appointing an RTI team and coordinator, scheduling intervention blocks, and determining a delivery model. Chapter 4 focuses on some of the processes of the implementation plan (see Figure 4.1), specifically how to analyze data and place students in appropriate intervention groups.

After CBM administration is completed, data analysis begins. Too often, this step is brushed over or not done thoroughly enough. Many schools across the United States now give *DIBELS* (*Dynamic Indicators of Basic Early Literacy Skills*, Good & Kaminski, 2002b) or *AIMSweb* (2010). If

Figure 4.1 Processes

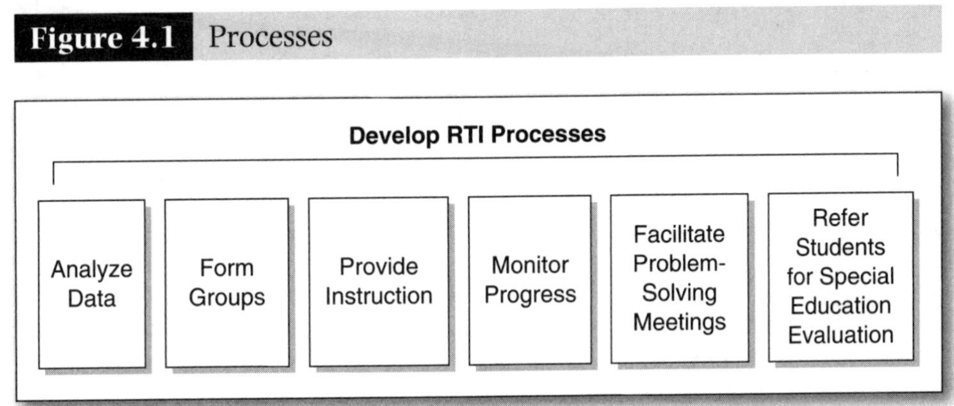

your school uses one of these assessments, rank your school's use of CBM data on a scale of 1 to 5 in Table 4.1.

Where does your school's use of data rank on this scale of 1 to 5? Do the teachers in your school know what the terms *error-pattern analysis, accuracy rate*, and *diagnostic screeners* mean? If not, then this chapter will provide some important information.

Schools that achieve significant gains in student reading scores have strategic data-analysis processes that are a foundation of their success; without strong data analysis, groups won't be focused. To illustrate why data analysis is essential, review the examples in Figure 4.2 and Table 4.2 in which two third-grade students attain the same oral reading fluency (ORF) score but should be placed in different groups based on the school's data-analysis practices.

Table 4.1 Rate Your School's Current Data-Analysis Procedures

Read the statements below and place a score of 1 to 5 in the spaces on the right. *1 = No awareness; 2 = Aware, but we don't do this; 3 = Some teachers do this; 4 = Most teachers do this; 5 = All staff use this procedure.*	
A. My school gives the assessment and conducts in-depth analysis of the data.	
B. We run reports and discuss results at grade-level meetings.	
C. We place students in groups based on yellow (strategic) or red (intensive) levels.	
D. We complete error-pattern analysis of CBM data and place students in groups based on similarity of errors.	
E. Based on accuracy rates on CBM indicators, my school identifies students who need diagnostic screener assessments and determines groups from CBM and diagnostic assessment data.	

Figure 4.2 Two Third-Grade Students With the Same Score and Different Needs

Example of Oral Reading Fluency Passage Student 1

My family went on vacation to the beach last summer. The first day was sunny, and we built sand castles with my uncle. My castle was a shark, and my sister's castle was a house with a moat.

When we got up the next morning, there had been a storm over night. The waves were so high that our castles were completely gone. My sister cried, but we decided to build more castles. This time, they were farther from the water.]

The next day, when the waves returned, they did not reach our new castles. Now every time we build sand castles, we know to build them far from the shore.

WRC = 80 **80/81 = 99% accuracy**

Example of Oral Reading Fluency Passage Student 2

My family went on vacation to the beach last summer. The first day was sunny, and we built sand castles with my uncle. My castle was a shark, and my sister's castle was a house with a moat.

When we got up the next morning, there had ~~been a storm over night. The waves were so high that~~ our castles were completely gone. My sister cried, but we decided to build more castles. This time, they were farther from the water.

The next day, when the waves returned, they did not reach our new castles. Now every time [] we build sand castles, we know to build them far from the shore.

WRC = 80 **80/98 = 82% accuracy**

Source: 95 Percent Group Inc. Reprinted with permission.

Table 4.2 Illustration of Different Data-Analysis Procedures

Data Analysis	Group Placement
School A: Example of minimal data-analysis procedures	
Teacher reviews classroom reports showing the score of 80 words correct per minute (wcpm) and recommendation level of strategic (yellow) for both students.	Both students are placed in the same fluency group because their scores fall within the same range.
School B: Example of strategic data-analysis procedures	
Teacher observes that both students are below benchmark on the classroom reports and then looks at scored passage probes to calculate accuracy rates. She also looks for any recurring error patterns.	*Student 1:* 99% accuracy • No further diagnostic assessment is needed. • Student is placed in a fluency group. *Student 2:* 82% accuracy • Student is screened with a diagnostic phonics screener in order to pinpoint skill deficits. • Student is placed in group for intervention in short vowels, long vowels, and so forth, depending on results of the phonics screener.

CURRICULUM-BASED ASSESSMENT

The main purpose of giving CBM assessments is to sort students for possible next steps. Collecting CBM data is comparable to this scenario: A nurse in an emergency room collects blood pressure, temperature, and pulse rate information from patients; she uses this data to determine who needs help first and which additional tests are needed to diagnose and provide a treatment plan for each patient. Just like the triage nurse determines next steps, teachers use CBM data to sort students for next steps. Which students need further testing with diagnostic assessments to pinpoint instructional needs? The data collected from a CBM assessment is inadequate for placing students in intervention groups. Placing students based on a yellow recommendation level leads to poor grouping decisions, as demonstrated with the two third-grade students who had the same score yet very different deficits. When schools determine grouping based solely on the red, yellow, and green recommendation levels, they are stuck at the "stoplight syndrome" stage. Instructional recommendation levels are a weighted average of several skills, which masks the details of the student's strengths and weaknesses.

When schools determine grouping based solely on the red, yellow, and green recommendation levels, they are stuck at the "stoplight syndrome" stage. Instructional recommendation levels are a weighted average of several skills, which masks the details of the student's strengths and weaknesses.

Consider CBM data a risk gauge or urgency indicator. Students whose instructional recommendation level is intensive are probably more at risk than those with a strategic indication, so seeing a student's scores highlighted in red should generate a sense of urgency. The instructional recommendation levels of intensive (red) or strategic (yellow) indicate that a student is at risk, but most of the time, they don't provide enough information about what to teach the student. For best results, you'll need to dig deeper into the data (see Figure 4.3).

Figure 4.3 Analyze Data and Form Groups

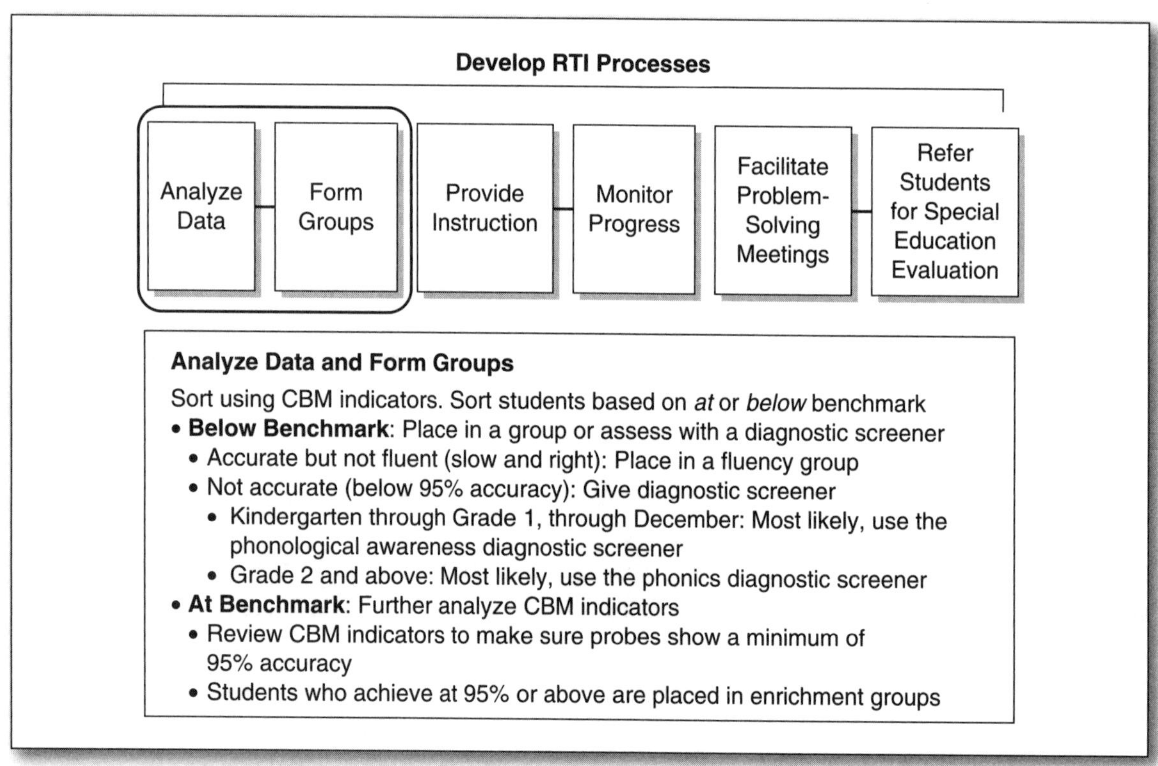

Often, students who scored below benchmark on ORF measures are placed directly into fluency groups. Teachers may observe that some students do well and their oral-reading scores take off, while others hardly improve. There's no time to waste for students and no extra room in intervention groups. Teachers need a way to know ahead of time which students will be successful in the fluency program. Those who improve in the fluency program read the words accurately but were too slow. Only below-benchmark students whose word-reading accuracy is 95% or higher on at least two of the three passages should be placed in the fluency program. Those below 95% accuracy need instruction on word reading before working on their fluency in connected text. This means that teachers have to look at the CBM probes and calculate accuracy rates rather than only reviewing the scores or instructional recommendation level.

Accuracy and Fluency

Teasing apart accuracy and fluency is a key step in an effective data-analysis process. As we taught this concept to teachers in workshops, we realized we needed a way to talk about fluency and accuracy so that teachers would be motivated to look at the probes. Although the four types of reading behaviors described in Figure 4.4 are simplistic, they carry an important message that sticks with teachers. We heard teachers talking about students' reading behaviors this way after the workshop, so we know the message has staying power.

Figure 4.4 Four Types of Reading Behaviors

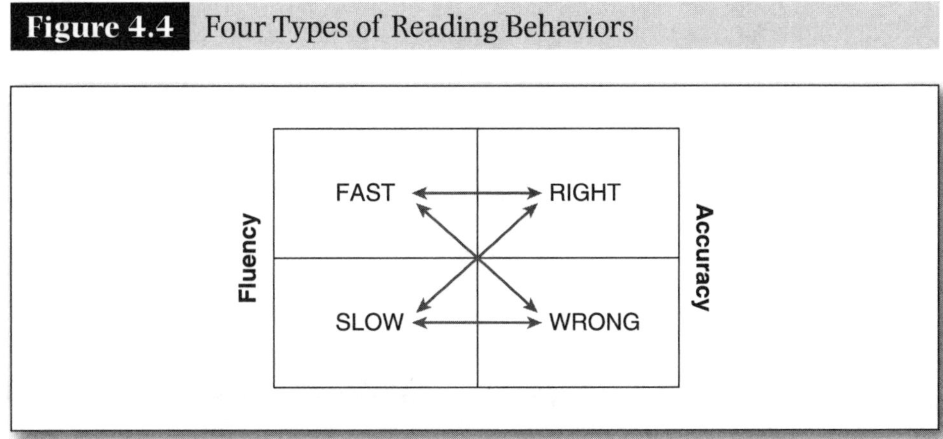

The figure displays fluency on the left and accuracy on the right. Notice that there are four boxes labeled with the four possible combinations of accuracy and fluency. We can think about behaviors that fall into each of these four boxes. Let's start with the analogy of a teenager learning to drive a car:

- *Slow and Wrong:* At first, every corner is a challenge because the teenager is not able to brake automatically, watch the other cars, find the turn signal and turn it on, and estimate how to keep from scratching the tires on the curb. It's not smooth because nothing is automatic, and this type of behavior usually causes the teenager to drive slowly. Before he can drive faster, he has to become accurate and automatic at the steps.
- *Slow and Right:* After some practice, the teenager is now becoming accurate with braking at the right time before the corner, finding the turn signal, turning it on without stumbling around, and keeping the tires the right distance from the curb. Now he's right, but he's not automatic enough with the subprocesses to go very fast.
- *Fast and Wrong:* Some teenagers who are fearless drive faster than they should before they are accurate with all the subprocesses. They adjust the radio while they are approaching a corner too quickly, and then they slam on the brakes too abruptly and barely stop in time. (These are the ones who make their parent's hair gray earlier!)
- *Fast and Right:* This is the teenager who has the components together (finally) and is accurate in estimating braking distances, distance between the tires and the curb, and location of the bumpers; she also can modulate acceleration to drive at the speed of traffic, making no mistakes (or very few—at least 95% of the time she's right).

Now let's apply these behaviors to reading. We are careful to specify that we're describing the reading behavior rather than the child because it would be insensitive to refer to a student as *slow and wrong*:

Fast and Right: Benchmark

- Example: Student scores 130 wcpm (words correct per minute) with an accuracy rate of 98%.
    - Score is above the required cut score of 110 for Grade 3.
    - Student reads with prosody, and comprehension is excellent.
    - Student is "pure benchmark" and is placed in an enrichment group.

Slow and Right: Strategic

- Example: Student reads 95% of the words correctly.
    - Assessment with a phonics diagnostic screener is not necessary.
    - Reading rate is too slow to reach benchmark.
    - Student is placed in a fluency group.

Slow and Wrong: Intensive

- Example: Student missed every fifth word (accuracy rate of 80%).
  - Student attempted 90 words in a minute (some correct and others incorrect) so fell below 110 wcpm.
  - Accuracy issues must be addressed before fluency issues.
  - Student is assessed with a phonics diagnostic screener and placed in the appropriate skill group.

Fast and Wrong: Benchmark or Strategic

- Example: Student read 145 words and got 112 right, just surpassing the 110 wcpm minimum.
  - The low accuracy rate of 76% means the student is at risk of not reaching benchmark in the future.
  - Student is assessed with a phonics diagnostic screener and placed in the appropriate skill group.

Sorting Students

The form in Figure 4.5 is useful to teachers, providing a way to sort students. Notice that at the bottom of each column, the next step is

Figure 4.5 Sorting Form

95% GROUP INC. Grouping Form Grade 3 Teacher Thrasher

	Fast and Right ORF	Slow and Right ORF	Fast and Wrong ORF	Slow and Wrong ORF
	WPM above 77 wpm and Accuracy 95% or above	WPM below 77 wpm and Accuracy 95% or above	WPM above 77 wpm and Accuracy below 95%	WPM below 77 wpm and Accuracy below 95%
	Blake	Samantha	Codey	Aaron
	Colby	Joshua	Daniel	Jonathon
	Sarah	Bryson	Zachary	Shanelle
	Sally	James	Lane	Victoria
	Mercedes	Savannah	Haley	Justin
		Kayla		
		Matthew		
Next Steps	Comprehension Instruction	Fluency Instruction	Phonics Screener for Intervention	Phonics Screener for Intervention
Lesson Format	Comprehension and Vocabulary Focus	Fluency Focus	Phonics Focus	Phonics Focus
Progress Monitor	*DIBELS* ORF	*DIBELS* ORF	*DIBELS* ORF and PSI Skill Level	*DIBELS* ORF and PSI Skill Level

Source: 95 Percent Group Inc. (2007a). Reprinted with permission.

indicated. Students in the left column need to be examined for potential comprehension issues. If comprehension is strong, then they can be placed in an acceleration or enrichment group. The next column to the right is for students who can be placed directly in a fluency group. The next step for students in the two right columns is to assess with a phonics diagnostic screener.

DIAGNOSTIC ASSESSMENT

In the sorting form in Figure 4.5, two groups of students need further assessment: those who are *fast and wrong* and those who are *slow and wrong*. There are three types of diagnostic screeners recommended, depending on the CBM indicators, grade level, and time of year:

1. Phonological awareness
2. Phonics
3. Comprehension

There are also students whose reading is severely impacted by low oral-language skills and minimal vocabulary. A diagnostic screener for vocabulary is not included here because we are not aware of any available vocabulary assessment that would enable teachers to place students in intervention groups. The types of comprehension screeners currently available assess students' mastery of specific comprehension strategies such as identifying main idea and cause and effect.

There are a number of phonological awareness and phonics diagnostic screeners available. The characteristics of a good diagnostic screener include the following:

1. Easy and quick to administer
2. Divided into separate skills to enable teachers to pinpoint mastery or deficit and to help in monitoring progress of a single skill
3. Uses pseudowords to evaluate decoding without inference of word recognition

When a kindergarten student is below benchmark on one of the phonemic awareness CBM indicators (e.g., phoneme isolation and phoneme segmentation), the next step is to administer a phonological awareness (PA) diagnostic screener. Several different PA diagnostic screeners are available. These diagnostic assessments are not normed or standardized because their purpose is to inform instruction. They also are not timed because they measure accuracy and not fluency; the CBM measures fluency, so they are all timed assessments.

When a Grade 2 or above student reads passages inaccurately, assessing each skill with a phonics diagnostic screener shows how well a student reads word patterns such as short vowels, long vowel silent-*e*, vowel teams, and *r*-controlled vowels. Many phonics screeners use pseudowords or pseudosyllables (or nonsense words or syllables) to assess how well a student reads syllables that represent a pattern; avoiding real words helps to ensure that the student didn't simply memorize the words.

Skill Continuums

It is helpful for the diagnostic screener to assess skills in the order of a developmental progression, or continuum, from simplest to most complex. The research evidence that PA skills develop along a continuum is strong, as summarized in the following excerpt from the *Report of the Early Literacy Panel* (National Institute for Literacy, 2009):

> Results from the analysis of findings in relation to PA appear to have instructional implications for early childhood educators. These findings suggest the importance of attending to children's progress along a developmental continuum of PA, rather than placing an emphasis on particular PA skills. . . . Rather than trying to teach a particular skill (such as phonological short-term memory), it may be of greater value to ensure that progress is occurring and that children are becoming progressively more able to deal with smaller and smaller units of sound (e.g., words, syllables, onset-rimes, phonemes). (p. 79)

The continuums we use for phonological awareness and phonics are shown in Figure 4.6.

All the PA skills should be mastered in kindergarten. Although *DIBELS* may show that a student at the beginning of first grade has not mastered phoneme segmentation fluency, it doesn't tell a teacher how far back to start instruction. The student may be lacking simpler skills—those that typically are mastered earlier in the development cycle.

The phonics continuum specifies the skills to be mastered by the end of first, second, and third grade. The continuum represents the bare minimum skill level expected in most core programs. For example, many published basal reading programs introduce vowel teams and *r*-controlled vowels in first grade. Both of these skills are shown as second-grade skills on the continuum because, even though they may be introduced in first grade, most programs spiral back and provide more instruction in second grade. By the end of second grade, a student should have mastered the skill of reading words with vowel teams

Figure 4.6 Phonological Awareness and Phonics Continuums

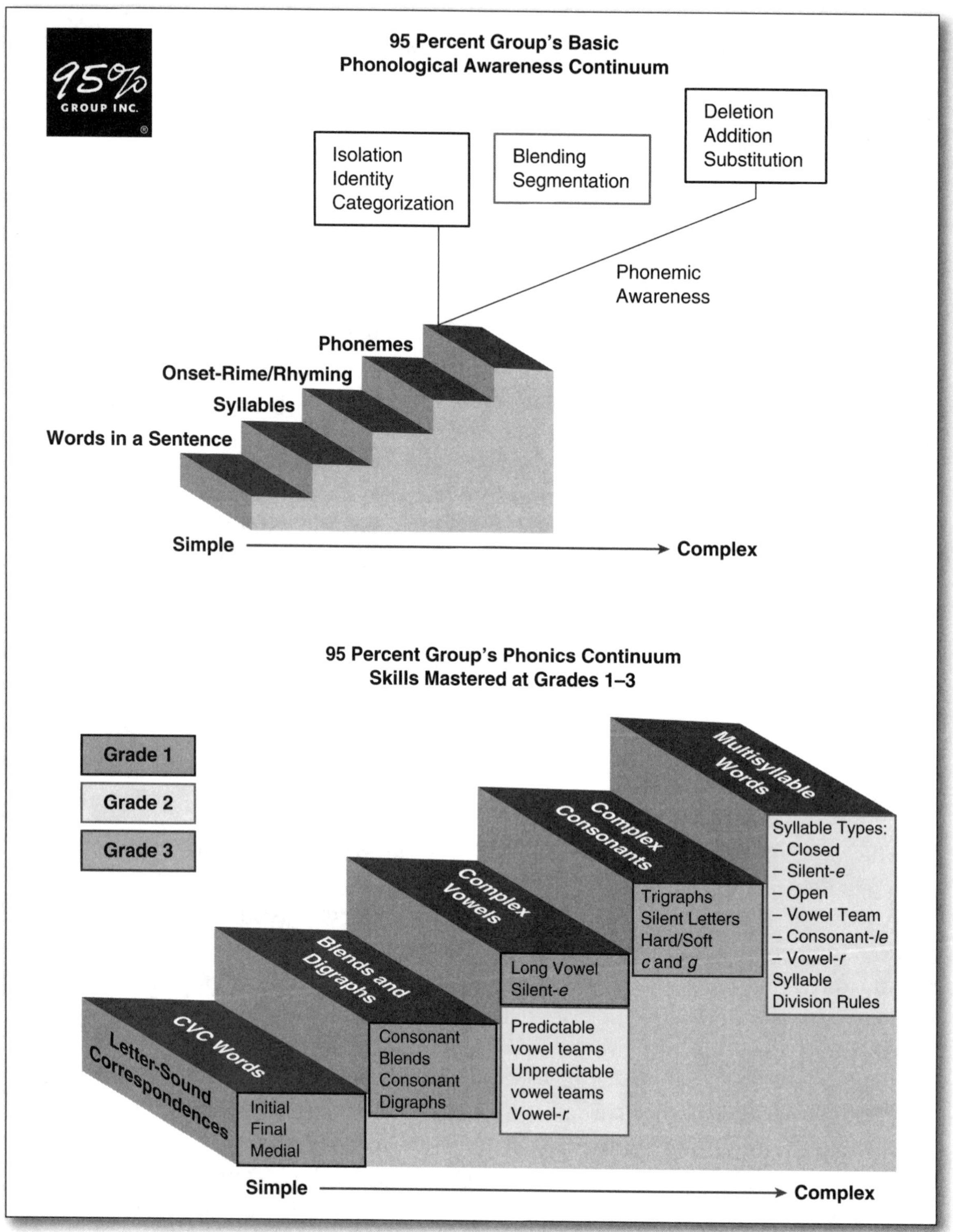

Source: 95 Percent Group Inc. (2005a, 2005b). Reprinted with permission.

and *r*-controlled vowels and be focusing now on learning to apply those single-syllable skills to multisyllable words. This continuum clarifies what is considered the bare minimum time by which students should have these skills mastered.

Using a Continuum Approach to Group Students

Using PA and phonics continuums allows teachers to see that students need to master skills in a predetermined order. Whenever a student struggles with a skill that is assumed to be mastered at a set grade level, he needs intervention. We recommend placing the student in a skill group to address the lowest skill not yet mastered but expected for his grade level. Then, after the student masters that skill, he should be moved to the next skill he fails to master on the screener. The advantage of using diagnostic screeners that align with a continuum of skills is that teachers can examine the diagnostic screener data to see which skills the student has already mastered and compare that to grade-level expectations, enabling a seamless process from the skill continuum to the assessment scores to grouping.

Using PA and phonics continuums allows teachers to see that students need to master skills in a predetermined order.

Another advantage of using a continuum approach to grouping is that the focus of the group is the name of the skill; instead of a *strategic* or *yellow* group, it's a *phoneme segmentation* group, a *long vowel silent-*e group, or an *open syllable* group. The focus of the group is clear in that instruction must be provided on this skill. Materials and strategies must support the instruction of that skill. In addition, there is no confusion about whether the groups are ability groups; it is clear that these are skill groups.

An example of the data collected on one skill of a phonics screener is shown in Figure 4.7.

Figure 4.7 Sample of Data Collected From Phonics Screener

Skill 3: Consonant Blends	
triz ~~flug~~ vug ~~blet~~ plit mond gamp	# Correct
~~strom~~ stom ~~splet~~ spit prant brund ~~grust~~ prest	5/10
Fred was *glad* to *swim* to the *raft* at *camp*.	# Target Words Correct
Brad held on to the *strap* so he could *jump* off the *stilts*.	10/10

Source: 95 Percent Group Inc. (2007b), p. A-4. Reprinted with permission.

PROGRESS MONITORING

A number of key questions arise when schools are establishing their progress-monitoring practices:

- Should we use our CBM or diagnostic screener for monitoring progress?
- How often should we monitor the progress of students?
- How can we manage all the data?

Assessment Tools

Selecting the appropriate assessment tool for progress monitoring depends on the group. The goal is to select the progress-monitoring instrument that most closely matches the focus skill of instruction. For some skills, the CBM is the best measure for progress monitoring. For example, the ORF indicators of the CBM are perfect for monitoring students in a fluency group. Measuring fluency by having students orally read alternate CBM passages for a minute enables teachers to observe whether the number of words correct per minute is increasing over time. On the other hand, students in fourth grade who are reading at a second-grade level and are working on mastering single-syllable vowel-team patterns should not be monitored with a CBM. Timing students as they read a fourth-grade passage that contains only a couple of words with vowel teams, and those are often embedded in three-syllable words, doesn't provide information on whether they are learning the skill that is the focus of instruction. Progress monitoring using the vowel-team section of the diagnostic phonics screener is far better because it informs instructional decisions about whether the student is learning that skill. Every so often, these students can be monitored with a CBM oral-reading passage, but the tool for the more frequent progress monitoring should match the skill that is the instructional focus. Using the CBM for regular progress monitoring can actually be discouraging for the student and the teacher; it's impossible to see progress.

The goal is to select the progress-monitoring instrument that most closely matches the focus skill of instruction.

Teachers appreciate using the phonics or phonological awareness diagnostic screeners for progress monitoring for several reasons. First, the diagnostic screeners illuminate whether the student is making progress on the *exact* skill that is the focus of instruction received in the intervention group. Second, the screeners are used to place the student in the group, and by using it also for progress monitoring, the teacher will know when to exit the student from the group. Finally, using diagnostic screeners for progress monitoring takes very little time. The teacher needs to assess the student on only one skill on the diagnostic screener, so it may take less than a minute. Students who don't pass the skill typically stay in the same group for another round of intervention instruction. For students who do pass the focus skill, assessment then progresses up the continuum until a skill is failed. At this time, the teacher can stop assessing because the skill not passed indicates the group the student should be placed in for the next round of intervention.

If your school uses this approach, make sure that the diagnostic screener provides at least two alternate forms along with the initial benchmark form. If your diagnostic screener has three forms, use Form A for the initial assessment and then alternate between Forms B and C for progress monitoring. For example, if a student is placed in the short-vowel group, use Form B to assess only short vowels for the first progress monitoring. Students who don't reach 90% on the pseudoword section (9 of 10 correct) stay in the group for another round of instruction. Then two weeks later, when it's time to monitor the progress of students again, use Form C of the same skill. If the student passes the skill, then continue to consonant blends with short vowels to see whether 90% is achieved on that skill. If not, stop assessing and use Form B for consonant blends to monitor progress in another two weeks. This cycle is illustrated in Table 4.3.

Table 4.3 Progress Monitoring and Regrouping Cycle

Date	Assessment Period	Form			Outcome	Group Placement
		A	B	C		
September 17	Initial Assessment	X			CVC: 40%	Place in the CVC group
September 30	Progress Monitoring 1		X		CVC: 90% Consonant blends: 50%	Move to the consonant blends group
October 14	Progress Monitoring 2			X	Consonant blends: 100% Consonant digraphs: 60%	Move to consonant digraphs group
October 28	Progress Monitoring 3		X		Consonant digraphs: 100% Long vowel silent-*e*: 30%	Move to long vowel silent-*e* group
November 10	Progress Monitoring 4			X	Long vowel silent-*e*: 50%	Keep in long vowel silent-*e* group
November 24	Progress Monitoring 5		X		Long vowel silent-*e*: 70%	Keep in long vowel silent-*e* group

Frequency of Progress Monitoring

Another common question concerns the frequency of progress monitoring. This decision can be made at the school level, but most of the time it is a district decision. The most typical frequency is every three weeks, but a two-week schedule is also common. Sometimes, although rarely, progress monitoring is done weekly, and in this case, most often it's only the students in the intensive, or red, zone who are monitored weekly. A monthly cycle is probably the bare minimum acceptable frequency.

Our recommendation is to start with a progress-monitoring frequency of every three weeks during the initial year of implementation, which will enable teachers to observe the changes because the measures are highly sensitive to small changes in performance. If schools monitor too frequently, too much time is taken from instruction. It's better in the initial implementation year to err on the side of monitoring less frequently because teachers are not sure how to use the data during the first couple of months—they have their hands full simply figuring out how to administer all the assessments, enter the data in the data-management system, access and interpret the reports, analyze the data, group and regroup, and plan instruction. Once the teachers have some of the other processes in place, they may (as a group) request that the schedule be changed to include more frequent progress monitoring.

If schools monitor too frequently, too much time is taken from instruction.

We recommend administering a progress-monitoring form to some of the students who score at benchmark one time between the fall and winter benchmarks and another time between the winter and spring benchmarks. Some schools rescreen all benchmark students, while other schools test only the "fence sitters," whose scores place them close to the cutoff. Using an alternate CBM for interim progress monitoring avoids any surprises in January and May.

Assessment Calendar

Consider creating an assessment calendar that shows the dates for the three benchmark CBM assessment periods, as well as the schedule for progress monitoring. Most schools allow two weeks for the fall, winter, and spring CBM benchmark screenings, where all students are tested, and a one-week window to complete the progress-monitoring testing. Since only the students in intervention groups are monitored for progress (except for the twice-yearly progress monitoring of benchmark students to avoid surprises), this testing can easily be completed in one week. Also, any teacher can decide to monitor the progress of an individual student more frequently. Sometimes, a student's scores will fluctuate wildly, and the only way to get an accurate progress line is to have more data points. An advantage of having a published assessment calendar is that it facilitates the planning of grade-level team meetings to regroup students to coincide with the latest available data. In the next section, the regrouping and progress-monitoring schedule is further explained.

REGROUPING CYCLE

Schools typically prefer to have a scheduled cycle for regrouping so that all the teachers at a grade level know what to expect. Let's consider the process of placing students in their initial groups assuming use of the walk-to-intervention model of grouping across the grade level. Initial grouping should occur immediately following administration of the CBM and the diagnostic screeners in September. Usually, the initial groups are created at a 45-minute meeting with all grade-level teachers present. Classroom teachers prepare a sticky note for each of their students by writing the student's name and lowest deficit-skill number on it. At the start of the meeting, all the skill numbers in the continuum are written as column headings on a whiteboard, and the sticky notes are arranged under these headings. This approach makes it easy for all the teachers to see how many students need each skill, which skills will need the most staffing, and how the entire grade level is distributed across the continuum.

One of the key tasks of grouping is to balance the group sizes given the staff available to teach groups. If there are eight staff members to teach groups during the intervention-block time (four classroom teachers and four additional intervention staff), then by the end of the planning period, the teachers must determine the best way to place all the students in the grade level into eight groups. The goal is to have large groups of benchmark and nearly benchmark students and the smallest groups for those students farthest below benchmark. Using sticky notes for this process is ideal because students can be moved into groups and adjusted until there is consensus. The final step is to assign staff to each group.

These initial groups meet for three weeks, and by the end of the third week, each intervention teacher completes the administration of a progress-monitoring assessment. The team may meet on Friday of the third week, with teachers arriving at the meeting with sticky notes again. Some students may need to stay another round in their current skill group, while others who passed the skill on the progress-monitoring assessment are ready to move up. This cycle of teaching for three weeks, progress monitoring at the end of the third week, and then regrouping based on

This cycle of teaching for three weeks, progress monitoring at the end of the third week, and then regrouping based on the most recent progress-monitoring results makes an easy system that teachers embrace.

the most recent progress-monitoring results makes an easy system that teachers embrace.

After some time, teams tend to move away from a periodic cycle to one that is more flexible. One school moved to a more fluid approach of making smaller changes weekly and then doing a major regrouping every six to eight weeks. Teachers monitor progress when they believe a student is likely to pass the skill and be ready to move to another skill. The team doesn't meet to regroup; instead, by Thursday at noon, all teachers post their updated progress-monitoring scores for any students they are exiting. Then, the reading coach looks at the "graduates" and moves them into new groups. If a group becomes too large, the groups—and potentially even staff assignments—are shifted, and then the new groups are posted back on the school's intranet by Friday morning at nine o'clock, giving teachers time to prepare for the new groups, which start on Monday morning.

Not only is it important for teachers to watch how the entire grade level is moving up, but they also need to analyze the rate of progress of individual students. If using a CBM for progress monitoring, such as for fluency, it's important for teachers to draw an aim line from the initial score to the benchmark cut score of the grade level. Then, each progress-monitoring point that falls below the aim line shows that the student's rate of progress is not sufficient. If the student's score falls below the aim line in three consecutive progress-monitoring periods, then the problem-solving team will have to look at ways to intensify instruction.

Progress Monitoring

Selecting the assessment instrument to use for progress monitoring makes all the difference in the RTI process. Using an oral reading fluency indicator to monitor whether a student in a long vowel silent-*e* skill group has mastered the skill is like using a pitcher to measure a teaspoon of a spice. It's the wrong tool for the job. When a student is in a phonics group, mastery of that specific phonics skill needs to be assessed in order to know when the youth is ready to exit that group. The oral reading fluency measure was not designed to measure individual phonics skills; its purpose is to serve as a quick indicator of overall passage-reading ability. There may be only one or two words containing a long vowel silent-*e* pattern in the portion of the passage that is read in a minute.

Using an oral reading fluency indicator to monitor whether a student in a long vowel silent-*e* skill group has mastered the skill is like using a pitcher to measure a teaspoon of a spice. It's the wrong tool for the job.

Consider one school's example of how its progress-monitoring data is used in regrouping decisions. This school's delivery approach at kindergarten is what they consider a modified walk-to-intervention model.

It's similar to a full walk-to-intervention model in that students who score below benchmark are placed in groups across the grade level; however, the students who are at benchmark stay in the classroom with assistants rather than go to one room. There are a total of nine groups taught by the five classroom teachers plus four interventionists. Intervention is provided five days a week for 30 minutes; the only exception is to cancel for field trips. They even complete progress-monitoring assessments outside of the 30-minute intervention block to avoid cutting into differentiation minutes. The groups each have two to five students.

This school has a clear cycle for progress monitoring and regrouping. At the beginning of the year, students were placed in temporary groups based on teacher observation before the CBM assessment window, which gave them an extra five weeks of small-group instruction. Later, when the *DIBELS* and diagnostic screener data were available, initial groups were formed. Students remained in these groups for three weeks; progress-monitoring data was collected by the end of week three and used to move students between groups, as needed. The three-week cycle continues, as shown in Figure 4.8.

Regrouping Schedule

Using a formal schedule for progress monitoring and regrouping is helpful especially during the first year of implementation. The advantage is that all staff know when to complete progress-monitoring assessments and when students change groups. Many schools move to an even more fluid regrouping process after the processes become intuitive. I'm reminded of a school that has a master data sheet available on the school's server, and teachers update their progress-monitoring data by Thursday at noon; the reading coach then posts any change in groups by Friday morning, and students move on Monday. This way, moving students from group to group is more flexible and fluent.

Figure 4.8 Grouping and Regrouping Cycle

	August	September	October	November	December
Skill Review	X	X			
Initial *PASI* or *PSI*		X			
New Groups Meet (Date)		Sept. 14	Oct. 5	Nov. 2	Dec. 7
Instruct		X	X	X	
Instruct		X	X	X	
Instruct		X	X	X	
Monitor Progress and Regroup		X	X	X	

SYSTEMS TO MANAGE THE DATA

With RTI, discussions about data occur at multiple levels:

- Data meetings with grade-level teams
- Data meetings between principals and reading coaches
- Data meetings between principals and individual teachers
- Problem-solving meetings, where the discussion focuses on individual students

Ready and efficient access to data reports is critical in RTI, so spending time up front to ensure efficient access to all the types of data reports needed is well worth it in the end.

After a couple of rounds of progress monitoring, there are a lot of data to manage between the CBM and the diagnostic screener scores. Most schools license use of a data-management system to capture their CBM data, which is available from the University of Oregon for *DIBELS* (Good & Kaminski, 2002b) data or from Pearson for *AIMSweb* (2010) data. Wireless Generation, who creates assessment systems to be used by educators, offers a system for *DIBELS* data collection on a tablet computer. The cost of these alternative CBM data-reporting systems varies tremendously, so it's critical to consider how to fund a preferred option over the long term after funded initiatives run out, such as Reading First or American Recovery and Reinvestment Act of 2009 (ARRA) stimulus money.

Schools also have to determine how to manage the data collected through informal diagnostic screeners. Some progress monitoring is done using the CBM, but more often, progress monitoring is done with informal diagnostic screener assessments. When monitoring the progress of students in intervention every three weeks (or more frequently), the data begins to pile up. Schools can either make or buy access to a data-management system for diagnostic screener data. Making such a system requires that teachers, reading coaches, or RTI coordinators develop spreadsheets; on the other hand, buying may include licensing access to a computer-based system for data reporting.

The data reports that a school will need include the following:

- View of point in time
  - Current and historical scores of all students by classroom, grade, school, or district
- Group placement
  - List of names of students in current groups
  - Recommended group placement (optional)
- Progress graphs by grade level
  - Historical view of the movement of students in a grade level through mastery of skills along a continuum

- Individual student reports
  - Graph of scores at various points in time, showing rate of progress in acquiring skills along a continuum
  - History of group placement by skill, including number of weeks per group
  - Size of group

The data-management system is important for both administrative and individual student decision making. From an administrative viewpoint, data is used in the following ways:

- The *district office* needs to ensure that students in each school are making progress. District staff members monitor the level and rate of student progress and initiate conversations with the principal of a low-performing school to identify factors inhibiting more robust student progress. In order to help with problem solving and to establish action plans, the data need to be viewed for each grade level at a school.
- The *principal of a school* needs to monitor student progress by grade level and by teacher. The principal can review the effectiveness of a grade-level team's practices by looking at the percentage of students reaching benchmark in kindergarten, first grade, and so on. A principal who reviews progress graphs of diagnostic screener data monthly will be able to flag and address issues before too much time elapses. Progress graphs from diagnostic screeners show the number of students who are working on each of the skills along the phonological awareness and phonics continuums.
- *Teachers* monitor not only the progress of the students in their own classroom at the periodic CBM periods but also the progress of individual students in mastering deficit skills along a continuum.

Coaches can print reports of overall progress for all students in the grade level, which will help the entire team see whether what they are doing is working or if there is a need for a substantive change. Data should be reviewed at least monthly so course corrections can be discussed. If the entire first-grade class is on a trajectory that won't reach the middle-of-year benchmark, then the whole team needs to talk about the structure. What can be changed? The following are factors that will impact the entire structure:

> Data should be reviewed at least monthly so course corrections can be discussed.

- Adding more intervention minutes to the schedule
- Dedicating more staff to reduce group sizes
- Improving instruction through additional professional development
- Acquiring more systematic materials

It is critical to have data to show the current level of student performance, the goal by midyear, and the gaps between the current level and the goal. In our experience, graphs that depict this data are the most valuable because they provide an at-a-glance big-picture view of the data. If the entire grade level's rate of progress isn't strong enough, then teachers need to brainstorm and make one or more of these changes. If some of the students are making excellent progress but others are not, then the changes to discuss will be more targeted.

Data reports for effective problem-solving meetings about individual students are also critical. Understanding a student's lack of response to appropriate and increasingly intense small-group intervention instruction is fundamental to determining whether a student may have a learning disability. The staff needs to demonstrate very clearly that the student received small-group instruction and that scores showed very little progress over time (especially in comparison to other students in the group). Other helpful information includes a history of the groups in which the student was placed and the intensity of instruction delivered in the groups. Intensity is a difficult thing to track; however, data to document increasing intensity includes placement in smaller group sizes and use of programs or materials that have more structure. Increased repetition cycles, excellent corrective feedback, and appropriate pacing is harder to document, but all are factors in increasing intensity of instruction.

Understanding a student's lack of response to appropriate and increasingly intense small-group intervention instruction is fundamental to determining whether a student may have a learning disability.

YEAR 1: SECOND HALF

Steps that should be taken during the second half of the first year are described in Table 4.4.

Table 4.4 Year 1: Second Half

Time Period	Assessment	Data Analysis and Grouping	Instruction	Problem-Solving Process
January **CBM winter benchmark (two-week window)**	Administer CBM to all students within the two-week time frame, and enter all data in CBM data-management system.	Analyze CBM data to determine which students need diagnostic screeners. Assess with diagnostic screeners (PA or phonics).	Continue teaching intervention groups during the two-week CBM-assessment window.	Meet with RTI coordinator to problem-solve any assessment issues (principal).

Time Period	Assessment	Data Analysis and Grouping	Instruction	Problem-Solving Process
Late January	Rescreen 10% of students randomly selected with a CBM alternate form (assessment team).	Analyze the random rescreening against the original. Address any issues.		
Late January—week after winter (MOY) benchmark	Administer diagnostic screener to any students newly designated as below benchmark, or inaccurate benchmark.	Analyze CBM and diagnostic data and place students newly found to be below benchmark in initial groups (teachers).		Attend grade-level team meetings to discuss data and when to bring students to problem-solving meetings (principal).
February	Continue administering progress-monitoring (PM) assessments with alternate forms. Use a diagnostic screener or a CBM to monitor progress; match the assessment to the skill group focus.	Continue regrouping. Move students who are at mastery level on progress monitoring up to the group for the next deficit skill.	Observe and coach intervention teachers.	After PM assessments, meet to discuss the progress rates of all students in intervention. Evaluate the overall effectiveness of groups (data team).
March	Assess students at benchmark once with CBM to avoid surprises.	Regroup at least monthly. Exit students to benchmark if there are at least two data points at that level.	Intensify instruction for students not making sufficient progress.	Bring individual students to a problem-solving meeting. Discuss potential referrals for testing for learning disabilities (teachers).
April	Continue periodic progress-monitoring assessments.	Continue reviewing progress-monitoring data and moving students.		Continue bimonthly or weekly problem-solving meetings; discuss student progress.

(Continued)

Table 4.4 (Continued)

Time Period	Assessment	Data Analysis and Grouping	Instruction	Problem-Solving Process
May end (EOY) benchmark	Administer the end-of-year (EOY) CBM benchmark assessment.	Analyze students for grouping in the fall. Consider summer school.	Evaluate Tier III materials and programs.	
June			Evaluate instructional materials for fall. Consider any summer institute PD for teachers.	Meet to discuss any revisions to the problem-solving process for next year (data team).
July	Make sure all materials for fall assessment are ready.		Prepare summer training materials.	

CONCLUSION

This chapter focused on a recommended set of data-analysis practices for a school. One of the intentions of this chapter was to clarify the purpose and uses of CBM data and to emphasize that they provide data in order to identify which students need diagnostic assessment. Separating accuracy from fluency is a key concept that teachers will need to understand in order to discover which students require diagnostic screening. We recommend using diagnostic screeners that follow a continuum of skills so that teachers can more easily transition from assessment to placing students in groups.

Additional materials and resources related to *Jumpstart RTI: Using RTI in Your Elementary School Right Now* can be found at http://my.95percentgroup.com/Jumpstart.

5

Delivering Effective Intervention Instruction

Chapter 3 focused on how to create the structures for procedures to support RTI, and Chapter 4 included information on analyzing data and placing students in the appropriate small groups. The focus of this chapter is on the characteristics that make intervention instruction effective. Intervention instruction is different from small-group instruction in the core reading block. It is, typically, even more focused on a skill area, especially one that should have been mastered previously; often, when a teacher pulls aside a small group during the core, it is to catch up students who were struggling with recent core-program instruction. Sometimes teachers assign students to work at literacy workstations while they pull a couple of students who were absent or were answering incorrectly during a whole-class lesson.

Intervention instruction can be described by a number of characteristics:

- Focus on pinpointed skills
- Students grouped based on deficits highlighted in diagnostic assessment
- Explicit, systematic, and sequential instruction
- Fast paced and engaging activities
- High level of student response

- Lots of practice
- Corrective feedback
- Sufficient practice to master a skill

The processes related to intervention instruction are depicted in Figure 5.1.

Figure 5.1 Provide Instruction

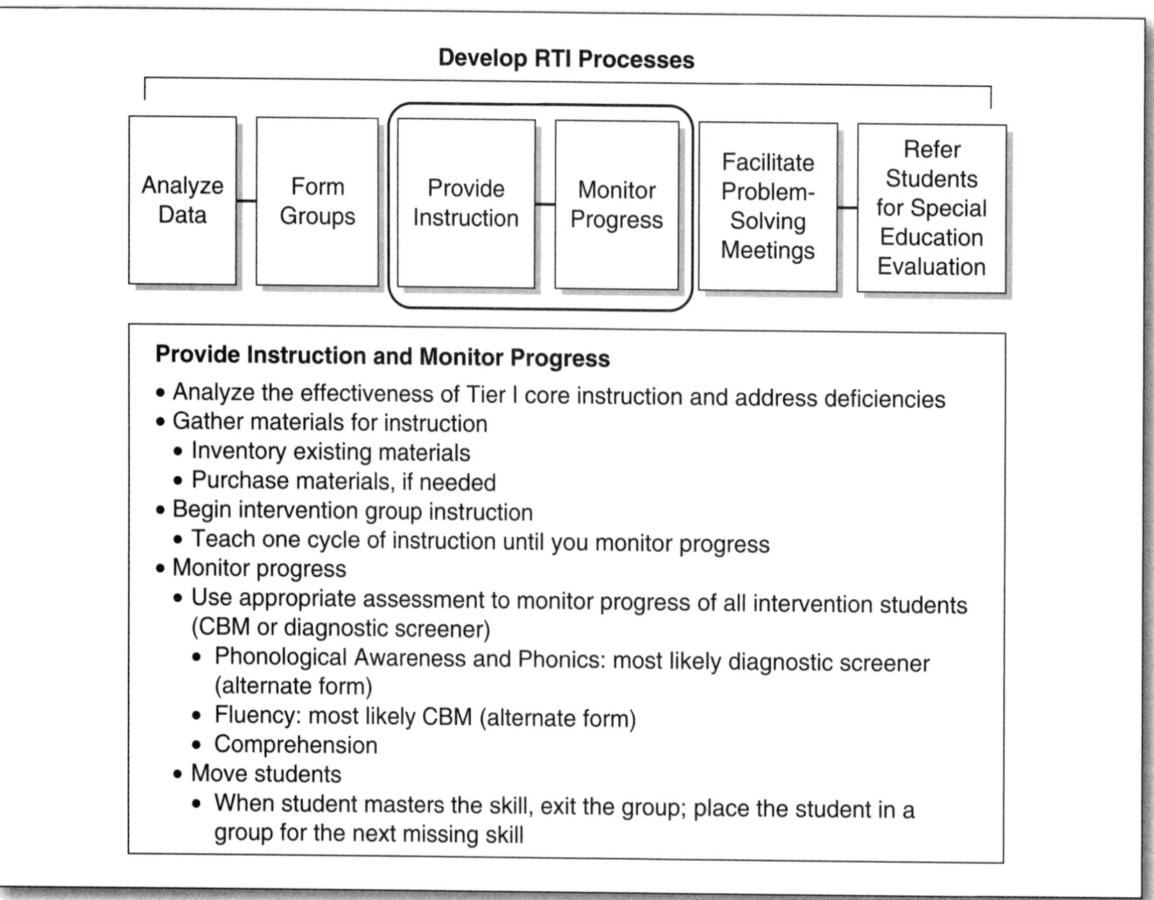

CHARACTERISTICS OF EFFECTIVE INTERVENTION INSTRUCTION

What does *explicit, systematic, and sequential* mean? Explicit instruction gives students information directly without the need for them to infer or guess to figure out what the teacher wants them to learn. Explicit instruction, for example, teaches students how to pull apart sounds in words, how to use knowledge of letter-sound correspondences to read words, and how to map sounds to print in order to write words. The modeling cycle of "I Do, We Do, You Do" is one of the most common ways to make instruction explicit. The teacher shows the student what to do (I Do), she then invites students to try it with her (We Do), and finally the students try it on their own while the teacher hovers to observe and intervene if necessary (You Do). A "think-aloud" process is often used to let students know what the teacher is thinking when figuring out a task or word pattern.

> The modeling cycle of "I Do, We Do, You Do" is one of the most common ways to make instruction explicit.

In contrast, nonexplicit instruction asks students to infer through exposure to words or text. For example, when presented with a list of words with the long vowel silent-*e* word pattern, students would recognize on their own that the pattern includes a vowel sound spelled with one vowel letter, followed by a single consonant, and then an *e* that is silent. Explicit instruction states the criteria that define that the vowel sound is long when the spelling pattern meets all three of those conditions. However, when students are expected to figure out words based solely on context or picture clues, the instruction is nonexplicit. Table 5.1 shows examples of explicit and nonexplicit instruction.

Table 5.1 Explicit Versus Nonexplicit Instruction

Nonexplicit (NE) Instruction	Explicit (E) Instruction	Contrast
Students are reading a book about the jungle. One student misreads the word *tiger*.	*"Yesterday we studied open syllable patterns and talked about how to divide when there is only one consonant between the vowels. Today we'll practice reading open syllables in multisyllable words."*	Instruction occurs incidentally in NE example. Instruction was preplanned and sequential in E example.
Teacher says, *"Read to the end of the sentence. Which word makes sense?"* Student doesn't answer.	Teacher holds up the word card for *tiger.* She underlines the *i* and *e*. Teacher says, *"There are two syllables. There is only one consonant between the vowels. The most common way to divide is between the* i *and* g.*"*	Teacher in NE example starts with text. She suggests using context clues. Teacher in E example starts with word instruction and later moves to application in text.
Teacher says, *"Look at the pictures. Do you see anything that might give a clue?"*	Teacher says, *"Watch me read the word.* Tī . . . ger. *I know the* i *is pronounced with the long sound because it's in an open syllable."*	Teacher in NE example continues to suggest clues. Teacher in E example continues with "I Do" portion of modeling.

(Continued)

Table 5.1 (Continued)

Nonexplicit (NE) Instruction	Explicit (E) Instruction	Contrast
Student still doesn't read word correctly. Teacher says, "*What letter does the word begin with?*" Teacher finally supplies the word, "*The word is* tiger. *Please continue reading.*"	Teacher says, "*Let's try one together. Look at the word* spider. *How many vowel sounds?* **(2)** *What do I underline?* **(*i* and *e*)** *Where do I divide it?* **(between the *i* and *d*)** *What are the two syllable types?* **(open, closed)** *Read the first syllable.* **(spī)** *Second syllable.* **(der)** *Put it together.* **(spider)**	Teacher in E example moves to "*We* Do" portion of modeling. Students respond to familiar set of questions. Teacher has been using this routine throughout instruction, so students can analyze the word and use their previously developed knowledge to successfully decode the word.
Students continue reading until one of them comes to another unknown word. Teacher repeats the pattern of questions about context clues.	Teacher gives students a passage that contains many multisyllable words with the open-closed syllable pattern, so they can practice applying the skill fluently and automatically.	In NE example, students don't learn techniques that will assure later success. In E example, text is used for practice in applying pattern knowledge explicitly taught previously, so students can become fluent and automatic and no longer need to go through the steps.

Note: Teacher dialogue is italic and in quotation marks; student responses are bold and in parentheses.

Systematic instruction, as the name implies, follows a system. The teacher follows procedures or routines when teaching so that students become accustomed to what to expect and how to follow along. Often, teachers use consistent gestures and a set of sound-spelling cards. For example, when cuing a student to remember the sound for short *i*, the gesture of scratching an itch on the forearm is used because *itch* is the keyword to help students remember the short *i* sound. Routine cards and lesson plans help teachers provide systematic instruction.

Routine cards and lesson plans help teachers provide systematic instruction.

An example of two gestures to show short- and long-vowel sounds are as follows: (1) For a short-vowel sound, use the pointer finger to point to the short vowel in a consonant-vowel-consonant word, and (2) for a long-vowel sound, use fingers in a V shape to demonstrate that it takes the vowel letter and the silent-*e* to spell the pattern and that they are separated by a consonant (see Figure 5.2).

Figure 5.2 Gestures Used in Systematic Instruction

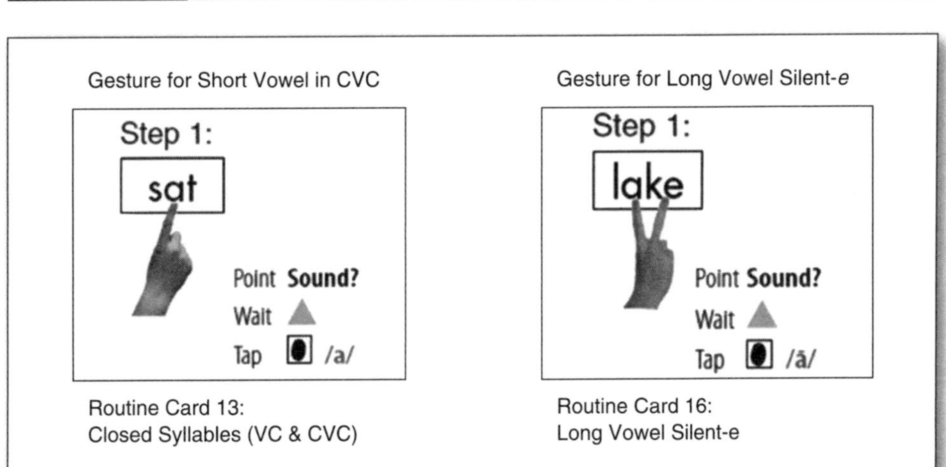

Source: 95 Percent Group Inc. (2008). Reprinted with permission.

Routine cards (Figure 5.3) help assure intensity and integrity of instruction. There are many advantages of teachers using routine cards:

- Support for teachers who don't know the pattern or strategy
- Reduction of teacher errors in describing a pattern or modeling a strategy
- Minimization of teacher talk
- Consistency among teachers who use the same gestures (important when students move to a different group)
- Assurance to administrators that the concept is taught correctly

In an ideal world, the same gestures are used in intervention groups as in the core program. If a school doesn't use a published core program, they benefit from using a generic version of routines that are not aligned to any particular published basal program. Some schools integrate these generic routines into Tier I instruction when their core program doesn't include types of gestures.

Sequential instruction means that skills are taught in a predetermined order or sequence. One sequence is articulated in phonological awareness and phonics continuums, as shown in Figure 5.4.

This example of a phonological awareness continuum contains three main areas: syllable, onset-rime, and phoneme. The skills are shown with a ladder graphic to communicate that they build from simplest to most complex (from the largest sound unit to the smallest). In this continuum, phonemic awareness is broken into eight more-detailed levels.

Syllables are the largest sound unit; for example, students learn to segment the separate syllables in the compound word *cowboy* into *cow*

Figure 5.3 Sample of 95 Percent Group's Routine Cards

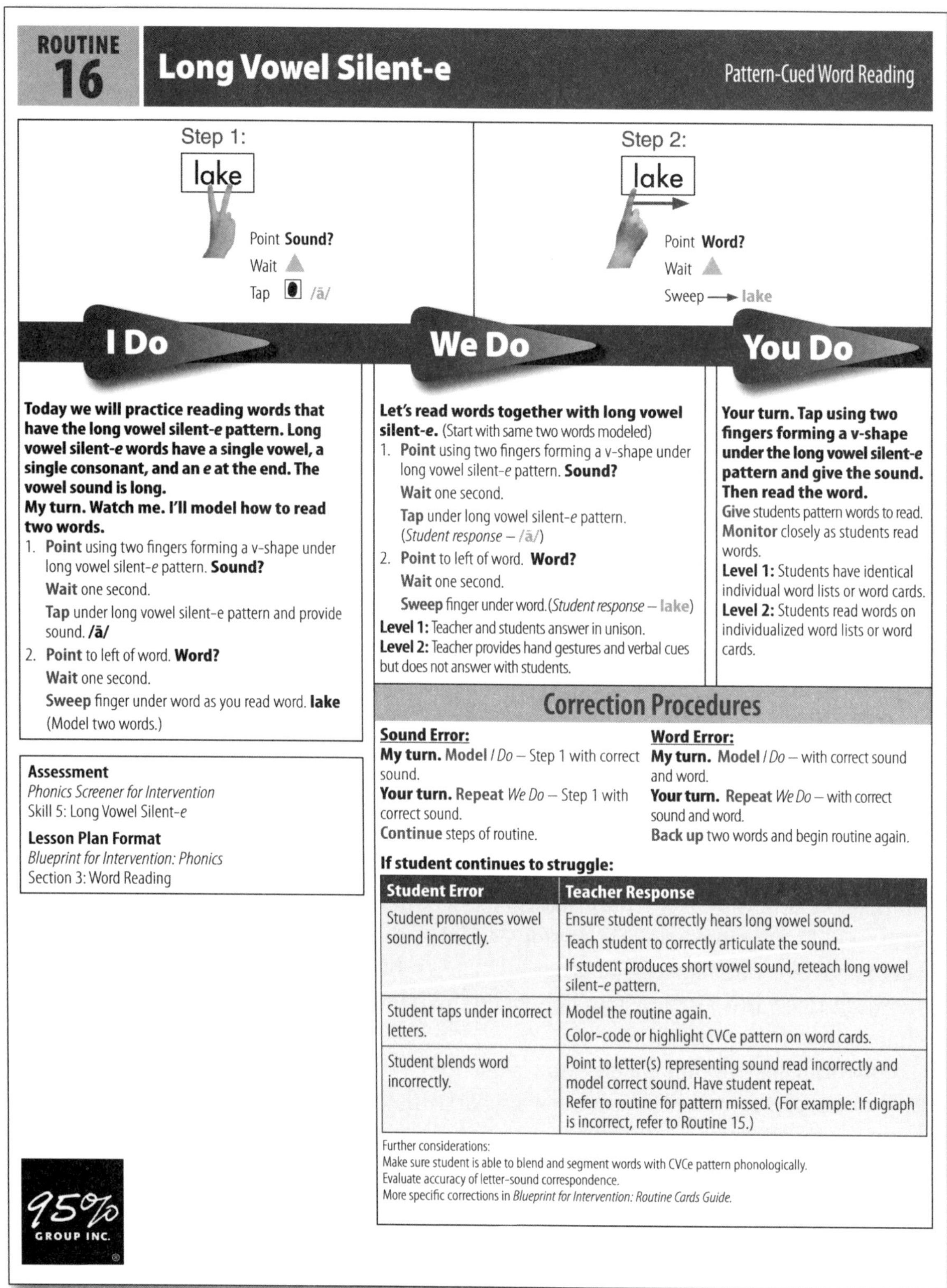

ROUTINE 16

Long Vowel Silent-e

Pattern-Cued Word Reading

I Do

Today we will practice reading words that have the long vowel silent-*e* pattern. Long vowel silent-*e* words have a single vowel, a single consonant, and an *e* at the end. The vowel sound is long.
My turn. Watch me. I'll model how to read two words.

1. **Point** using two fingers forming a v-shape under long vowel silent-*e* pattern. **Sound?**
   Wait one second.
   Tap under long vowel silent-e pattern and provide sound. **/ā/**
2. **Point** to left of word. **Word?**
   Wait one second.
   Sweep finger under word as you read word. **lake**
   (Model two words.)

We Do

Let's read words together with long vowel silent-*e*. (Start with same two words modeled)

1. **Point** using two fingers forming a v-shape under long vowel silent-*e* pattern. **Sound?**
   Wait one second.
   Tap under long vowel silent-*e* pattern.
   (*Student response* – /ā/)
2. **Point** to left of word. **Word?**
   Wait one second.
   Sweep finger under word. (*Student response* – lake)

Level 1: Teacher and students answer in unison.
Level 2: Teacher provides hand gestures and verbal cues but does not answer with students.

You Do

Your turn. Tap using two fingers forming a v-shape under the long vowel silent-*e* pattern and give the sound. Then read the word.
Give students pattern words to read.
Monitor closely as students read words.
Level 1: Students have identical individual word lists or word cards.
Level 2: Students read words on individualized word lists or word cards.

Assessment
Phonics Screener for Intervention
Skill 5: Long Vowel Silent-*e*

Lesson Plan Format
Blueprint for Intervention: Phonics
Section 3: Word Reading

Correction Procedures

Sound Error:
My turn. Model *I Do* – Step 1 with correct sound.
Your turn. Repeat *We Do* – Step 1 with correct sound.
Continue steps of routine.

Word Error:
My turn. Model *I Do* – with correct sound and word.
Your turn. Repeat *We Do* – with correct sound and word.
Back up two words and begin routine again.

If student continues to struggle:

Student Error	Teacher Response
Student pronounces vowel sound incorrectly.	Ensure student correctly hears long vowel sound. Teach student to correctly articulate the sound. If student produces short vowel sound, reteach long vowel silent-*e* pattern.
Student taps under incorrect letters.	Model the routine again. Color-code or highlight CVCe pattern on word cards.
Student blends word incorrectly.	Point to letter(s) representing sound read incorrectly and model correct sound. Have student repeat. Refer to routine for pattern missed. (For example: If digraph is incorrect, refer to Routine 15.)

Further considerations:
Make sure student is able to blend and segment words with CVCe pattern phonologically.
Evaluate accuracy of letter-sound correspondence.
More specific corrections in *Blueprint for Intervention: Routine Cards Guide.*

Source: 95 Percent Group Inc. (2010). Reprinted with permission.

Figure 5.4 Phonological Awareness and Phonics Continuums

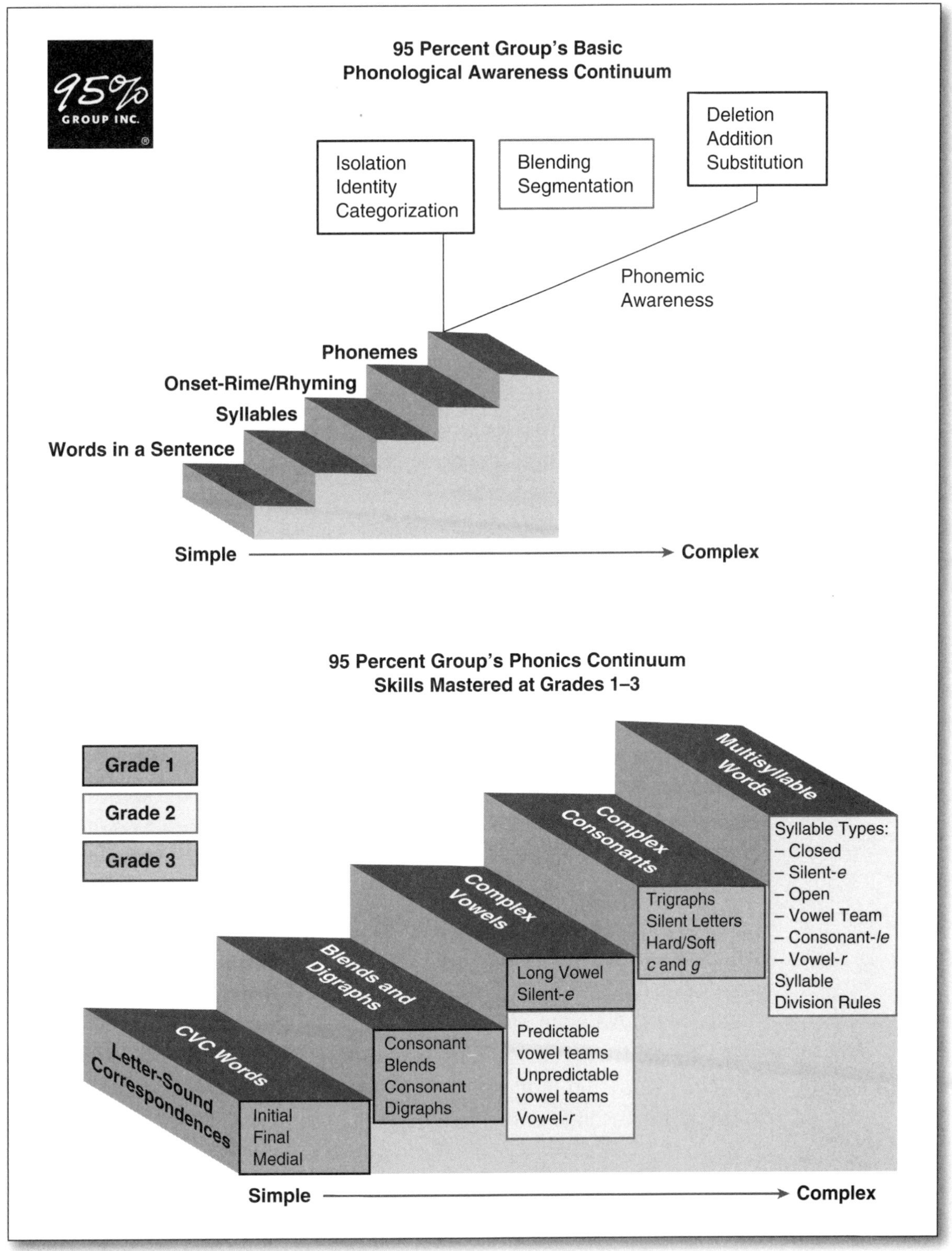

Source: 95 Percent Group Inc. (2005a, 2005b). Reprinted with permission.

and *boy.* This skill is easier to teach than some others because teachers can demonstrate to students who struggle that it's possible to sense the number of syllables by noticing the number of times that their chin drops to say the vowel. This helps make the abstract unit of a syllable more concrete.

Dividing words between the onset and rime level is more challenging than segmenting at the syllable level. Learning to segment words between the onset and rime is more important than simply learning how to distinguish and produce rhyming words. Students who can flexibly adjust one sound and create another word will more easily work with word families later.

The phoneme level is divided into three levels. The first level (isolation, identification, and categorization) focuses on one phoneme, typically either the beginning or ending sound. Students who can tell you, for example, that the first sound in the word *bat* is /b/ have demonstrated the skill of initial phoneme isolation. Identification is the skill of identifying whether more than one word has the same sound: "Do *fix* and *fall* start with the same initial sound of /f/?" Categorization is not only the ability to segment the first sound from multiple words but also the ability to compare the first sounds and determine whether they all fit in a category: "Listen to these three words: *cat, cup, coat,* and *sock.* Which one doesn't fit?" Categorization at the phoneme level is sorting by one sound. Both identification and categorization require a mastery and application of isolation.

The second phoneme level includes phoneme blending and segmentation. Both of these skills require awareness of all the sounds in the word, not just the initial or ending sound. To master this skill, students need to be able to put sounds together to make words and to pull sounds apart when given a spoken word.

The highest phoneme level is manipulation, which includes addition, deletion, and substitution. Addition is adding one sound to make a new word (e.g., from *cat* to *scat*). Deletion is taking away a sound to make a new word (e.g., *spark* to *park*). Substitution is the most complex phonological task. An example of a phoneme substitution task follows: "Say *rug*. Change the /r/ to /t/. What's the new word?" (Tug)

This task is difficult because it incorporates several lower skills. A student must isolate and delete the first sound in *rug* (/r/), add /t/ to the beginning, and then blend the new word *tug*. The complexity of this task demonstrates that the continuum provides a sequence or order of instruction in skills in that a more complex one depends on mastery of lower skills. While benchmark students can learn these skills in a more random order and switch from skill to

While benchmark students can learn these skills in a more random order and switch from skill to skill within the continuum, students who struggle benefit from a more sequential approach of mastering one skill at a time before moving up the continuum.

skill within the continuum, students who struggle benefit from a more sequential approach of mastering one skill at a time before moving up the continuum.

The phonics continuum is similar to the phonological awareness continuum. On the bottom is a very detailed progression of single-syllable skills, starting with basic and moving to advanced concepts. The skills considered as basic are mastered by the end of first grade. These include all the short-vowel patterns plus one long-vowel pattern. The short-vowel patterns include CVC (consonant-vowel-consonant) and short vowels with consonant blends and digraphs. The first long-vowel pattern is typically the most consistent and recognizable: long vowel silent-*e*. Advanced phonics concepts include more difficult vowel patterns (vowel teams, *r* vowels) plus complex patterns, such as silent letters (*kn*, *gn*) and trigraphs (*dge* spells /j/).

Using a skills continuum is a critical component of intervention instruction based on the principle of differentiating for missing skills. With effective diagnostic assessment, teachers can identify which skills a student has mastered and which ones are missing in order to avoid wasting time on what is already known. As one of my colleagues says, "The alternative is to equip teachers with a 50-pound phonics program and require that all students complete all lessons from 1 through 99, whether they need them all or not." The sequence within the continuum allows teachers to assume mastery of skills earlier in the continuum and simply continue to review them.

All program materials have a sequence, whether they are core or Tier II or III. What's important is to identify the sequence, even if it's not made transparent in a table or chart. Several of our client schools have purchased phonological awareness materials that provide teachers with a spiral-bound set of short lessons. I've observed many teachers using these materials to provide whole-class daily instruction for about 20 minutes with kindergarten and first-grade students. As I watched the students, it was very obvious to me that the materials were perfect for the "haves" but unsuitable for the "have nots." Each day, instruction moved between multiple levels of phonological awareness. The teacher read from the guide and prompted students with a set of syllable tasks, followed by phoneme substitution, followed by onset-rime, and so on. Notice how those skills hop around on our phonological awareness continuum (Figure 5.4). For the benchmark students whose phonological awareness skills were normally progressing, the material provided great practice. For the struggling students, the random sequence made learning nearly impossible. The tasks were coming at them in rapid succession without allowing for practice of one task until mastery was achieved before moving to a more complex skill. These materials are not effective for small-group intervention instruction because the lessons are constructed without a sequence building from simplest to most complex and do not contain sufficient explicit instruction and modeling.

Pinpointed and Focused

Instruction that is differentiated by skill group is pinpointed and focused. It does not cover all five components of reading instruction. Imagine each 30-minute lesson including all five components of reading. The teacher would spend six minutes on phonological awareness, six minutes on phonics, six minutes on fluency, six minutes on vocabulary, and six minutes on comprehension. This doesn't make any sense for a couple of reasons. First, not all students in the group need instruction in each of those areas. Second, the instruction time is so diluted that teachers can't help students make enough progress in any one area. If it takes the entire 90-minute reading block to effectively teach all five components of reading, then how could it be possible to teach all five components in a 30-minute intervention lesson? If too many students are missing multiple components, then it's more effective to supplement the Tier I core instruction so that fewer students need Tier II intervention on those components. Tier II is only for students who have skill gaps.

Instruction that is differentiated by skill group is pinpointed and focused.

While instruction is focused on one particular skill, it doesn't mean that it can't include another component. For example, in a lesson for kindergarten students that is focused on phoneme segmentation, often a five-minute review of letter names can be added if there is evidence from the diagnostic data that the students need this skill as well. In another example, for a lesson on the *oi-oy* vowel team, the teacher should take 10 to 20 seconds to define the word *foist* that appears on a word card and in one of the passages. When the students finish reading the decodable passage, teachers should ask a few comprehension questions to check for understanding.

Fast Paced

Effective pacing of intervention instruction is one of the hallmarks of a teacher who is fluent with the modeling, gestures, and routines of instruction. Intervention has to be paced in such a way that students benefit from multiple opportunities to respond. Effective intervention instruction allows students to respond seven times a minute. Before teachers panic, I'll clarify what I mean by *respond.* When students respond, they may be reading or writing a word but may also be underlining a vowel, highlighting a word with the target pattern, raising fingers to segment the sounds in a word, moving a chip or letter into sound-spelling boxes, or raising a thumb to indicate hearing the target sound in a word. Not all parts of the lesson will be paced the same:

During the I Do, the students aren't responding at all, yet during the We Do and You Do cycles, the students should be responding more than seven times per minute.

> Effective pacing of intervention instruction is one of the hallmarks of a teacher who is fluent with the modeling, gestures, and routines of instruction.

Pacing is not only related to response cycles, but it's highly correlated to the level of engagement. When the instruction is too slow, it's more likely that the students' attention will wander. Also, if teachers are talking too much and not asking enough questions, it's too easy for students to become passive and to disengage.

When the pacing of the instruction is too slow, the first thing a reading coach should examine is where in the lesson the teacher bogs down and spends too much time. Is her I Do too wordy? Does she spend too much time asking questions? ("Sound?" is better than "What's the sound?") Developing fluency in intervention instruction is like developing fluency in playing tennis. To improve, it's critical to break the game down and focus on the components that are not smooth. A tennis player may need to have a trainer observe his form to help him improve. Similarly, principals or reading coaches can use observation to help teachers improve their instruction. One of the most satisfying days in my schedule is when I provide walk-through training for principals on how to use an intervention-snapshot observation form to distinguish good and poor instruction and to use that information to coach teachers to improve instruction.

Corrective Feedback

The students in intervention groups are the ones who are obviously making mistakes during whole-class instruction, yet it's impossible to stop and respond to each mistake because the teacher must teach to the mean of the class. However, these students need corrective feedback each time they make a mistake in the small group. Teachers must model the lesson again. The I Do, We Do, You Do cycle is not linear; it's circular, and there are loops back and forth like the chutes and ladders on a board game. After a teacher moves from an effective I Do to the We Do, observing and listening will reveal whether students are ready to move to the You Do. If students aren't answering everything correctly at the We Do stage, circle back to modeling another I Do. Then, only after a successful We Do, move to the You Do stage.

It's imperative that the teacher is able to closely observe how each student is responding to questions so that no mistake goes uncorrected. That's why group size matters. Yet there are no hard-and-fast rules about the exact size of the group because that depends on the focus skill. For a phonological awareness group with kindergarten students who must all be moving the manipulatives, most likely the groups cannot exceed five in number and three students may be even better. For a third-grade fluency group, it may be possible for one teacher to instruct 20 students effectively. The 30-minute block might start with a minilesson that includes demonstrating one aspect of fluency followed by dividing the students into pairs to take turns practicing while the teacher circulates around the room to guide each pair.

> It's imperative that the teacher is able to closely observe how each student is responding to questions so that no mistake goes uncorrected. That's why group size matters.

Plenty of Practice

Students who are struggling need ample opportunities to practice until they reach mastery. During the core instruction, students don't get sufficient corrective feedback, close observation, and enough practice cycles to master a skill. The number of necessary repetition cycles varies by student. For some students, three times of practicing is enough; for other students, it may take up to 20 times or more to master a skill. The most effective intervention instruction is structured so that all participants in the group are responding together rather than taking turns. That's one reason that intervention groups are not quiet places; students quickly learn that while they are supposed to raise hands during whole-class instruction, they don't need to raise hands during this time. All students are responding to all questions. And if the teacher is listening to one student read a passage aloud, then the other students are continuing to whisper-read a different part of the passage until the teacher moves around the semicircle to listen to each of them.

In an article about what inspires students to want to practice something enough to master it, Kathleen Cushman (2010) talks about how she studied the activities and passions that captured the attention of teens. She observed and interviewed teens about their quest to perfect skateboarding, violin, dancing, chess, or sports skills. There is increasing evidence that opportunity and practice have more influence on performance of most things than innate ability. She writes about the importance of the right kind of practice, which has to be at just the right level so that the student won't face failure and want to give up. An excerpt from her article follows:

> There is increasing evidence that opportunity and practice have more influence on performance of most things than innate ability.

> The students were describing, we realized, what cognitive researchers like K. Anders Eriksson call *deliberate practice*. Their learning tasks were set at a challenge level just right for them. They repeated a task in a focused, attentive way, at intervals that

> helped them recall the task's key elements. All along, they received and adjusted to feedback. (p. 53)

This is what we want in intervention groups. Teachers need to have small enough group sizes to be able to set the tasks at just the right challenge level and provide corrective feedback followed by deliberate practice activities that will lead to mastery.

OTHER CONSIDERATIONS

There are several areas of confusion that are addressed in this section; for example, teachers may believe that using activities represents an effective approach to teaching an intervention group. Teachers may also question the value of lesson plans or be uncertain about areas such as fluency, vocabulary, comprehension, and acceleration.

The Role of Activities in Intervention Instruction

One intriguing question is whether teaching a set of activities is equivalent to teaching an explicit lesson. In an earlier book, *I've DIBEL'd, Now What?* (Hall, 2006), the focus is on activities. The book was popular because teachers love the activities; but did it lead to student gains that were the most robust possible?

Let's compare a sample activity for phonological awareness from the Florida Center for Reading Research (FCRR, 2008) K–1 Student Center Activities to illustrate instruction for the same skill:

Option A: Example of student activity for phoneme substitution at a literacy workstation

- Student uses a worksheet that has 10 boxes for 10 examples. Within the boxes, there is a target picture to the left and two alternative pictures to the right. Work is completed independently at a literacy workstation. The student listens to the teacher give the task on a prerecorded audiotape, stops the tape and circles the answer on the worksheet, starts the tape to hear the instructor give the second task, and so forth, until all 10 tasks are completed.
- The teacher's recorded instructions tell the student to listen to each word, follow the directions, and then say the new word. One example is given orally without access to pictures. The teacher instructs: "Say the word *cat*, change the /k/ to /h/, and say the new word (hat)." The student is then directed to start the tape and go to the next picture.

- The worksheet has a picture of a fan on the left with a choice of a can or pan on the right side. The task is "say *fan*. Now, change the /f/ to /k/. Say the new word."

Option B: Example of explicit instruction on the concept of phoneme substitution

- The teacher has a mat with an arrow at the bottom and four blue circles and one red circle at the top of the mat.
- Instruction begins with the following explanation:
  - We're going to learn to change one sound in a word to make a new word.
  - Watch me. My turn. The word is *mug*. I'll change /m/ to /b/ to make a new word.
  - I pull a circle down for each sound in mug, /m/ . . . /u/ . . . /g/. (The instructor pulls a blue circle to the line as each sound is said.)
  - I slide my finger along the line and say the word *mug*.
  - (The instructor points to the circle that represents /m/.) I want to make a new word by changing the /m/ to /b/.
  - I'll push the /m/ sound up. I'll use the red circle to represent the new sound /b/. (The instructor pulls the red circle down to the beginning.)
  - I'll say the /b/ sound here. (The instructor points to the red circle.)
  - I slide my finger along the line and say, /b/ . . . /u/ . . . /g/. The new word is *bug*.
- Instruction continues with the teacher progressing to the We Do and inviting students to answer with her until they can answer alone.
- Then, each student receives a mat and circles and completes You Do examples with as many words as needed to master the skill.

The preceding activities are categorized as *phoneme manipulation*, which is not very specific because manipulation tasks can be addition, deletion, or substitution. Phoneme substitution is changing one sound to another to make a new word. Because in Option A the teacher is not seated at the student workstation, there is no one to monitor whether the student has completed the task correctly. The choices of the alternate pair are rhyming words, so the teacher's audiotape has to be really clear and well pronounced for the student to get it correct.

The examples above contrast an activity and explicit teacher-directed instruction; however, it's not that one option is better than the other. Each has a purpose and a proper place. If the teacher provides the explicit instruction with students until they master the skill, the activity is a perfect next step for practice. For students who struggle, the activities alone without the explicit instruction won't enable skill mastery as efficiently as when explicit instruction in the skill is provided first and the activity is used for students to practice *after* they know how to do it. The activities can bring engagement and variety to the end of the lesson. A word of caution: Be sure that teachers know how to select activities that are exactly the same skill as the explicit instruction. In addition, they need to select activities that give as much opportunity for all the students in the group to answer.

If the teacher provides the explicit instruction with students until they master the skill, the activity is a perfect next step for practice.

Let me give an example about opportunities to practice: Recently, I was conducting a principal's walk-through to observe intervention instruction during the 30-minute block. One of the teachers was using a board game. There were four students seated at the kidney-shaped table with her. One student used a spinner with numbers, advanced his marker, and then looked at the letter on the board. Then, the teacher said a word that started with the letter. The student's job was to segment sounds in the word while all the other students watched, many of whom were instead looking around the room daydreaming. Because of the time it took for students to spin the spinner, count out the places, say the letter, and respond to their word, there were only seven words covered in seven minutes. Since each child was responding individually, they each only manipulated a maximum of two words in seven minutes. Compare this to a different activity that would require each student to respond every time, so they each could have responded seven times in a minute.

The Value of Lesson Plans

To be systematic, lesson plans are a key tool, especially for teachers who are new to teaching a skill. The plan encompasses the system for teaching a skill. It includes all the steps and provides a consistent structure. Good lesson plans also assist in providing sequential instruction because they are designed so that teachers can spiral back and review previously taught skills.

Presented next are two examples of lesson plans developed for use with a Tier II intervention group. The first one is a phonics lesson, and the second (Figure 5.5) is a phonological awareness lesson. This phonics lesson plan, based on 95 Percent Group's (2009) *Blueprint for Intervention: Phonics* (2007) and the *Phonics Lesson Library* (2009), has six steps:

Step 1: Review a previously mastered skill.

- Prepare students to focus on the new skill by reviewing a previously taught skill. This step is like a warm-up. For example, when the new skill is consonant digraphs, review short vowels in CVC words. Or instead of practicing an earlier skill on the continuum, work on sight-word fluency or review a high-level phonemic awareness skill before teaching a phonics skill.

Step 2: Teach a new concept.

- This is when the teacher explicitly teaches the new skill. For example, long vowel silent-*e* words have a single vowel, a single consonant, and an *e* at the end, and the vowel sound is long. A gesture of V-shaped fingers is used to call attention to the pattern. The teacher uses the I Do, We Do, You Do modeling cycle.

Step 3: Word Reading

- Students practice reading words that contain the pattern. The goal is for students to become accurate and fluent at the word level.

Step 4: Word Building

- Students practice encoding words that contain the pattern using sound-spelling paper and markers with whiteboards or pencil and paper.

Step 5: Sentence Dictation

- Students write a teacher-dictated sentence that contains pattern words along with sight words and words that contain patterns that appear earlier on the continuum.

Step 6: Passage Reading

- Students transfer their newly learned skill to reading passages that contain multiple examples of the pattern words so that they continue to practice reading words. It's important for students to read decodable text that contains an unusually high number of words containing the target pattern along with only previously mastered patterns and known sight words.

The two examples show phonological awareness and phonics lesson plans. The following sections explore the type of instruction that may be taking place in some of the other skill groups for Grade 1 and above.

Fluency

For students who read at least 95% of the words correctly but who are not at the benchmark oral-reading level, placement in a fluency group will help them improve their reading rate.

For students who read at least 95% of the words correctly but who are not at the benchmark oral-reading level, placement in a fluency group will help them improve their reading rate. Fluency work is included in other groups at the subskill level; for example, the phoneme segmentation group practices

Figure 5.5 Sample of 95 Percent Group's Phonological Awareness Intervention Lesson

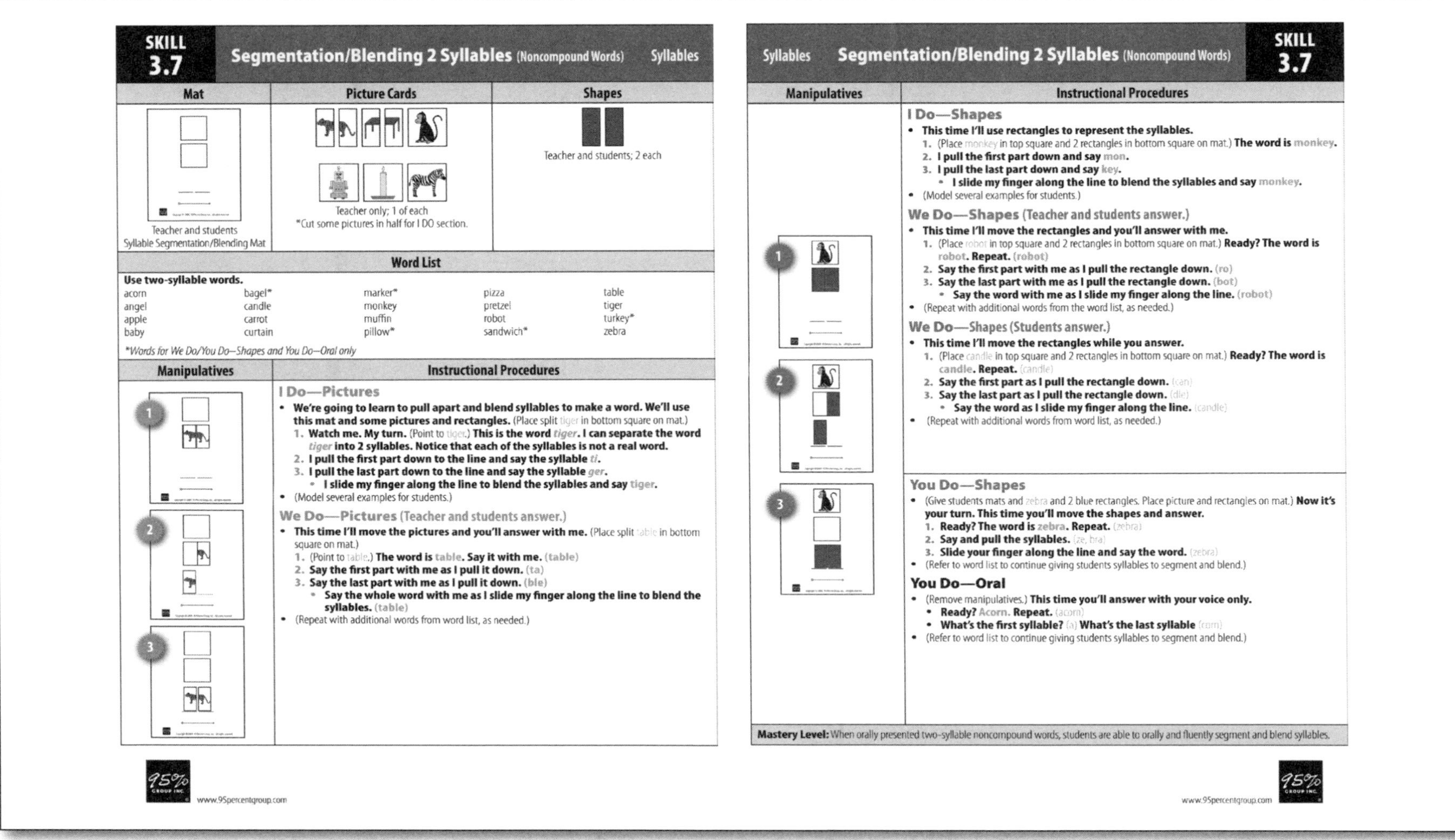

SKILL 3.7 **Segmentation/Blending 2 Syllables** (Noncompound Words) Syllables

Mat	Picture Cards	Shapes
Teacher and students Syllable Segmentation/Blending Mat	Teacher only; 1 of each *Cut some pictures in half for I DO section.	Teacher and students; 2 each

Word List

Use two-syllable words.

acorn	bagel*	marker*	pizza	table
angel	candle	monkey	pretzel	tiger
apple	carrot	muffin	robot	turkey*
baby	curtain	pillow*	sandwich*	zebra

**Words for We Do/You Do—Shapes and You Do—Oral only*

Manipulatives | **Instructional Procedures**

I Do—Pictures

- **We're going to learn to pull apart and blend syllables to make a word. We'll use this mat and some pictures and rectangles.** (Place split tiger in bottom square on mat.)
  1. **Watch me. My turn.** (Point to tiger.) **This is the word *tiger*. I can separate the word *tiger* into 2 syllables. Notice that each of the syllables is not a real word.**
  2. **I pull the first part down to the line and say the syllable *ti*.**
  3. **I pull the last part down to the line and say the syllable *ger*.**
     - **I slide my finger along the line to blend the syllables and say tiger.**
- (Model several examples for students.)

We Do—Pictures (Teacher and students answer.)

- **This time I'll move the pictures and you'll answer with me.** (Place split table in bottom square on mat.)
  1. (Point to table.) **The word is table. Say it with me.** (table)
  2. **Say the first part with me as I pull it down.** (ta)
  3. **Say the last part with me as I pull it down.** (ble)
     - **Say the whole word with me as I slide my finger along the line to blend the syllables.** (table)
- (Repeat with additional words from word list, as needed.)

www.95percentgroup.com

Syllables **Segmentation/Blending 2 Syllables** (Noncompound Words) **SKILL 3.7**

Manipulatives | **Instructional Procedures**

I Do—Shapes

- **This time I'll use rectangles to represent the syllables.**
  1. (Place monkey in top square and 2 rectangles in bottom square on mat.) **The word is monkey.**
  2. **I pull the first part down and say mon.**
  3. **I pull the last part down and say key.**
     - **I slide my finger along the line to blend the syllables and say monkey.**
- (Model several examples for students.)

We Do—Shapes (Teacher and students answer.)

- **This time I'll move the rectangles and you'll answer with me.**
  1. (Place robot in top square and 2 rectangles in bottom square on mat.) **Ready? The word is robot. Repeat.** (robot)
  2. **Say the first part with me as I pull the rectangle down.** (ro)
  3. **Say the last part with me as I pull the rectangle down.** (bot)
     - **Say the word with me as I slide my finger along the line.** (robot)
- (Repeat with additional words from the word list, as needed.)

We Do—Shapes (Students answer.)

- **This time I'll move the rectangles while you answer.**
  1. (Place candle in top square and 2 rectangles in bottom square on mat.) **Ready? The word is candle. Repeat.** (candle)
  2. **Say the first part as I pull the rectangle down.** (can)
  3. **Say the last part as I pull the rectangle down.** (dle)
     - **Say the word as I slide my finger along the line.** (candle)
- (Repeat with additional words from word list, as needed.)

You Do—Shapes

- (Give students mats and zebra and 2 blue rectangles. Place picture and rectangles on mat.) **Now it's your turn. This time you'll move the shapes and answer.**
  1. **Ready? The word is zebra. Repeat.** (zebra)
  2. **Say and pull the syllables.** (ze, bra)
  3. **Slide your finger along the line and say the word.** (zebra)
- (Refer to word list to continue giving students syllables to segment and blend.)

You Do—Oral

- (Remove manipulatives.) **This time you'll answer with your voice only.**
  - **Ready? Acorn. Repeat.** (acorn)
  - **What's the first syllable?** (a) **What's the last syllable** (corn)
- (Refer to word list to continue giving students syllables to segment and blend.)

Mastery Level: When orally presented two-syllable noncompound words, students are able to orally and fluently segment and blend syllables.

www.95percentgroup.com

Source: 95 Percent Group Inc. (2009), pp. 96–97. Reprinted with permission. All rights reserved.

separating the sounds in words rapidly and effortlessly. The groups for each phonics skill practice reading words with the target pattern, until students can accurately and quickly recognize the pattern and pronounce unfamiliar words. This section refers to the work of an intervention group that is focused on increasing fluency at reading sentences in passages of connected text. Repeated reading of the same passage is a frequently used research-based practice to increase fluency. First, a student times an unrehearsed reading of a passage (often called a cold read). The child then listens to an audiotape and practices rereading the text. Finally, after practice, the passage is read and timed again and scores are compared. Across the weeks, cold-read times on new passages should increase. There are other fluency-building strategies, but because of its efficiency and effectiveness, repeated reading should be the key strategy supplemented with others for variety.

Vocabulary

Research has shown that to improve a student's vocabulary, a multicomponent approach is necessary. *Bringing Words to Life* (Beck, McKeown, & Kucan, 2002) has informed the practice of many teachers on how to wisely choose words to teach from a storybook. The authors recommend that teachers define the unfamiliar words with student-friendly definitions followed by experiential learning activities for students to fully absorb what a word means. It will take much more than teaching a set number of new words per week to close the gap for students who have low oral-language and vocabulary skills. Teachers also need to encourage and model word consciousness and self-teaching strategies so students know how to use clues to figure out unknown words. Michael Graves's (2006) *The Vocabulary Book* explains the need to include several components for an effective vocabulary curriculum and not rely solely on teaching words. Many schools view vocabulary as an area of need for so many of their students that they integrate supplemental instruction into their core Tier I time. They then pull students who are ELL (English language learners) for extra time on oral-language development.

It will take much more than teaching a set number of new words per week to close the gap for students who have low oral-language and vocabulary skills.

Comprehension

Recent research has shown that teaching students comprehension strategies is effective. However, Daniel Willingham (2006/2007) and others have raised questions about how extensively these strategies are taught in schools today. What I tell teachers is "a little dab'll do ya" when it comes to comprehension strategies. (Those of us over 50 may remember this was the advertising line for Brylcreem, a men's hair gel.) Willingham asserts that students can learn strategies for comprehension such as main idea, cause and effect, and others, with only a few lessons. After limited instruction and practice in teaching comprehension strategies, a teacher will better spend time teaching students to grapple with the meaning of the text and to learn to read in more-thoughtful questioning ways. Another way to state it is to teach students to approach reading with a problem-solving perspective rather than to focus on gaining information to complete a graphic organizer.

Teach students to approach reading with a problem-solving perspective rather than to focus on gaining information to complete a graphic organizer.

Acceleration or Enrichment Groups

For students who have reached benchmark, many schools offer acceleration or enrichment groups in which the curriculum is above and beyond what's in the Tier I core program. Students read text that is above grade level and participate in literature circles, author studies, or writing in response to reading. While observing in schools during intervention time, sometimes we'll see these groups doing activities. The best way for students to spend this differentiated time is by reading and responding in meaningful ways to what they have read. There's no need for fancy curriculum; it's all about time on text. Parents are very excited about having their children's needs met as well. RTI is about differentiation for *all* students—not just those who are behind.

INTERVENTION MATERIALS AND PROGRAMS

There is a great deal of confusion about the role of intervention materials and programs. It seems that this confusion may have emerged from two influencing factors. First, many articles and books about RTI talk about the *protocol approach*: Students are placed in a purchased program that uses one specific protocol (that is, the one-size-fits-all program and all related materials are purchased as a whole by the district) and that is to be taught with fidelity. Second, when Reading First rolled out across the country, the federal government focused on *research-based materials.*

Protocol Model

The protocol model of RTI is often positioned in contrast to the problem-solving model. The protocol model is where schools purchase one or two specific intervention programs and any student who scores below benchmark is placed in one of these programs. With this approach, the data-analysis stage is limited because placement is into a standard curriculum and there is limited need for meetings about changing student placement. Progress monitoring is done in order to move students from the protocol program for Tier II to another program for Tier III. The protocol approach is very different from the approach described in this book, which is that Tier II is more effective when diagnostic screeners are used to pinpoint skill gaps and students are placed in small groups based on specific skills.

There are several key issues with the standard protocol approach. First, it assumes that all students who score below benchmark are missing the same skills. In addition, the programs tend to be designed in a more comprehensive way to include more skills, probably because it's assumed that students with varying deficits will be in the same groups. For example, a program may include letter naming, letter-sound correspondence, and the entire phonological awareness continuum wound together throughout the weeks of lesson plans. It's a bit like taking entire strands from a core program and teaching them rather than pinpointing where the student is deficit.

Problem-Solving Model

Based on experience from early in my career using the protocol model, the data shows lower student gains than the gap approach. Schools must provide the support and training needed for a school staff to learn how to implement the more-challenging gap approach. The approach in this book is that Tier II intervention instruction should be targeted and focused, and students should receive instruction only on the skills they are missing and skip assignment to skills they have mastered. Each group is focused on more discrete skills on the continuum—the individual steps rather than the entire PA continuum. The materials needed for the gap model are very different from those needed for the standard protocol approach. The reason to purchase intervention materials and programs is to save teachers time. Programs don't teach; informed and skilled teachers teach intervention groups. The best materials for Tier II instruction using the diagnosed gap approach can be decoupled, so teachers can teach specific lessons rather than being forced to teach all of the lessons in order. Fidelity is about teaching the instructional strategies that are effective and outlined in the materials rather than following a script verbatim.

> Tier II intervention instruction should be targeted and focused, and students should receive instruction only on the skills they are missing and skip assignment to skills they have mastered.

Research-based program is a term that is highly misunderstood. All publishers call their programs and materials scientifically based these days. Purchasing a program with a gold stamp that says "research based" gives about as much assurance as a food product claiming to be "lower in fat." Of course, everyone is jumping on the bandwagon to improve sales of their products. However, consider what it would take to scientifically research an intervention program. Students would have to be extensively matched for other influencing factors, randomly assigned to the focus program or at least one other alternative, receive no other reading instruction or exactly the same core instruction, and be taught by teachers who follow the programs without any variation to the script. It's impossible to scientifically research intervention programs because students cannot be denied the core program (or the core cannot be controlled that carefully) while studying the effect of just the intervention materials.

Instead of acquiring research-based programs, schools should use materials that include research-based instructional strategies.

Instead of acquiring research-based programs, schools should use materials that include research-based instructional strategies. For example, the strategy of teaching phoneme segmentation using a move-it-and-say-it mat and circles is research based and should be included in materials or programs that are used in intervention instruction. In the initial phase of your RTI implementation, a good step is to ask teachers at each grade level to inventory the materials and programs the school already has. Most of what you will need you already have, probably stockpiled in closets and storage bins. RTI is not about purchasing a lot of new materials; it's about repurposing what you already have and organizing it for use by intervention teachers. Some schools organize materials by skill name from the continuums and place them in bags in a book room to be checked out weekly and returned each Friday. Others use their school's server to store electronic files with teacher-created lessons that follow a standard lesson-plan format, organized in folders by continuum skill names. One district reading coordinator made the following comment about materials:

> At the beginning, I thought intervention was "stuff." Along the way, I realized that intervention is not stuff. It is explicit, purposeful teaching. It's harder and involves teaching differently than you've ever done. We don't need the games. We need to know the deficits.

Having described the materials needed for Tier II, consider how Tier III may be different. Students in Tier III intervention groups are typically missing more skills across the entire continuum and do not simply have gaps. They tend to be far behind, many times by several grade levels. Following a program in Tier III makes sense because the students need to learn all the skills; therefore, a comprehensive program that includes plenty of practice fits with the need. When it comes to Tier III, fidelity to the program has more meaning. These students have to be evaluated for possible testing for a learning disability if Tier III instruction doesn't work. Therefore, it's important to see whether their scores improve after instruction in a Tier III program—for an extra hour a day in a small group of no more than three students.

Interventions for English Language Learners

> The diagnostic screeners and the intervention materials need to be adapted rather than translated to acknowledge the phonological differences between the primary language and English.

Students learning English as a second language benefit from the same approach recommended throughout the book. Diagnostic assessment in their primary language is critical in order to identify phonological and phonics deficits. Schools have seen huge growth in the bilingual population by teaching phonological awareness to kindergarten and first-grade students in their primary language. The diagnostic screeners and the intervention materials need to be adapted rather than translated to acknowledge the phonological differences between the primary language and English. After students are moved to receive core language arts instruction primarily in English, their intervention should mirror the language of the core instruction. Once the student's core instruction is primarily in English, the intervention can be offered in English, also.

As instruction begins, so does progress monitoring. Schools tend to make two common mistakes when it comes to progress monitoring:

1. Assessing too frequently: When teachers are first getting RTI going, it is far better to assess every three weeks instead of weekly. Too much time is lost on assessments before teachers are really using the data. After a few months, teachers will be ready to consider which groups of students should be monitored for progress biweekly or weekly.
2. Assessing with the wrong tool: To monitor progress and determine whether the instruction is working, the teacher needs to use the assessment that measures the skill that is the focus of instruction. Many times, progress monitoring with a phonological awareness or phonics diagnostic screener is much more effective than assessing with a CBM.

CONCLUSION

A set of characteristics that describe effective intervention instruction were provided in this chapter, as well as the modeling cycle of I Do, We Do, and You Do, which helps make instruction explicit. It's important to remember that a continuum of skills, which defines a sequence for instruction, is a critical component of intervention instruction. And lesson plans and routine cards are beneficial in ensuring that instruction is systematic. Activities should be used for practice after explicit and systematic instruction is provided in a sequence.

6

Initiating a Problem-Solving Process

In nearly every document written about RTI, problem-solving meetings are mentioned, yet often without providing adequate information about what these meetings really look like. There are two terms often used interchangeably: *data team meetings* and *problem-solving meetings*. I'll start by clarifying the terminology. In this book, the term *problem-solving meeting* is reserved for discussions about an individual student and how to address that specific student's lack of progress in acquiring deficient skills. The term *data team meetings* will mean two other types of meetings. First, *data meeting* is a term often used to refer to the conversations about the progress of an entire grade level of students; however, I'm proposing that this is a dialogue that should be part of a typical grade-level team meeting and not something that occurs at a special meeting. Finally, in this book, the term *data team meeting* encompasses the dialogue of the RTI team about the status of the implementation of the entire building, including processes that are standardized and coordinated across all grade levels.

GRADE-LEVEL TEAM MEETINGS

The content of grade-level team meetings has been evolving in many schools. One driving force may be the advent of professional learning communities (PLCs), which have improved what team meeting discussions should entail. The trend is to move away from administrative details ("administrivia") toward dialogue about curriculum, data, and student learning. Many of the administrative details, such as whether enough parent volunteers have been recruited for the next field trip, are handled via e-mail. Grade-level team meetings, often called collaboration meetings, are now focused on instruction and may even include a study of a professional book that all teachers are reading and discussing together.

In addition to richer discussions at grade-level team meetings, much has changed in regard to assessment. Increased assessment and accountability is a topic that individual teachers seem to either emphatically embrace or despise. Regardless of whether a teacher likes or dislikes assessment, it seems here to stay. The No Child Left Behind Act of 2001 (NCLB) requires all states to participate in national assessments, such as the National Assessment of Educational Progress (NAEP), and states now require the administration of CBMs as universal screeners. Kindergarten through Grade 2 teachers, once outside the high-stakes testing years, are now expected to assess with early literacy screeners. It's in the school's best interest to encourage teachers to discuss assessment data in their team meetings. RTI provides a natural way to embed the data discussions into grade-level team meetings.

The data that should be discussed at a grade-level team meeting relates to the entire grade level more than to an individual student. Teams should start by evaluating where their students are at the beginning of the year and reflecting on the implications of the data for their upcoming year. For example, if the first-grade team sees that more than 60% of the students will enter the year below benchmark in phoneme segmentation fluency (PSF), a skill students should have mastered by the end of kindergarten, there will be huge implications for staffing intervention groups in the fall. Likewise, if the fourth-grade team discovers upon closer analysis that 70% of the students who score below benchmark have accuracy rates below 95% on their oral reading fluency (ORF) scores, staff will need to allocate time for assessing with a diagnostic phonics screener. Once the team members have pinpointed the skills that students lack and have placed students in groups, they will need to analyze whether they have the materials and training to deliver instruction to the phonics intervention groups.

> The data that should be discussed at a grade-level team meeting relates to the entire grade level more than to an individual student.

Data begins to permeate discussions after teachers become more comfortable interpreting it. After the first year, grade-level teams should be asked to set goals of where students should be by the middle and end of the year. This is typically accomplished by looking at the percentage of students at benchmark, strategic, and intensive. Ask the grade-level team to draw the triangle (see Figure 6.1) for the beginning of the year and then draw another one with their midyear goal. One school placed a bulletin board in the hallway of each grade level and updated it to show

Figure 6.1 BOY and MOY Triangles

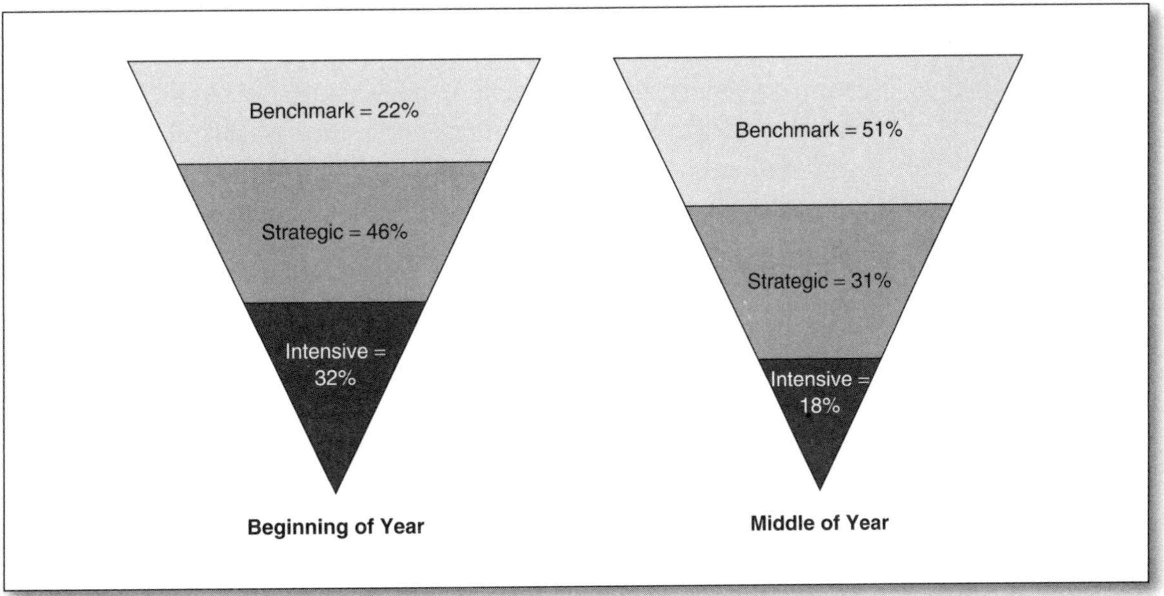

the number of students reaching benchmark throughout the year. Whenever I was in that school, it reminded me of United Way's thermometer-shaped progress graphs, which are filled in as they make progress toward reaching a fundraising dollar goal.

One of the RTI outcomes mentioned earlier in this book is the paradigm shift of teachers referring to "our kids" instead of "my kids"; looking at data for the entire grade-level supports this change of view. Using data walls is another important way team members can periodically check on student progress. Data walls also are critical for motivating teachers to hold the course when things get tough. Many teams use a science project board and fold it up in between meetings to keep the student data confidential.

In addition to checking on the percentage of students reaching benchmark, team members have a number of other important topics to discuss at grade-level team meetings. Teachers need time to talk about whether all aspects of the RTI implementation are working and brainstorm alternative procedures if something isn't running smoothly. Team members sometimes decide that progress monitoring monthly is not frequent enough, and now that they've learned the process, they'd like to change the progress-monitoring frequency to every three weeks. After months of meeting as an entire team to regroup students using sticky notes on a board, team members may decide that they're ready for a process that takes less team-meeting time and enables moving students weekly instead of every three weeks. For example, teachers can update progress-monitoring data on the school server by Thursday noon, so the

RTI coordinator can post the revised group assignments on Friday, and new groups can start Monday morning. Every student will be monitored for progress at least every three weeks, but monitoring can be more frequent if the teacher believes that a student is ready to exit the current skill group and move up to the next deficient skill.

Grade-level team meetings can provide a time to talk about whether too many students seem to be getting "stuck" for more than one round of intervention at a particular skill level. If that happens, the team needs to address several questions:

- Is the instruction provided for this skill explicit enough?
- How can instruction be intensified?
- Are the skill groups small enough?
- Does the team have access to materials that help teachers provide effective instruction on this skill?
- Is more professional development on this topic needed?

Data changes everything in these meetings. It focuses the team on student achievement and provides a foundation for meaningful professional dialogues about student success.

Data changes everything in these meetings. It focuses the team on student achievement and provides a foundation for meaningful professional dialogues about student success.

PROBLEM-SOLVING MEETINGS

The focus of a problem-solving meeting is on an individual student whose progress is not sufficient. All staff members who work with this student gather to discuss the insufficient rate of progress and then decide the steps that can be taken to provide further support. These meetings should be short and efficient. After spending a few moments examining the data to verify how low the student's rate of progress is, the team's discussion focuses on what's been provided so far and what else can be done to intensify intervention instruction. The problem-solving meeting is the meeting in which decisions to move a student from Tier II to Tier III are made. In addition, this is the meeting in which any decision to refer a student for possible testing for special education services is made within the RTI framework (see Chapter 7, "Referring a Student for Special Education Testing").

The problem-solving meeting is the meeting in which decisions to move a student from Tier II to Tier III are made.

Meeting Attendees

Given the focus on making decisions about a student's intervention instruction, it's important to have all the right people in the room for a problem-solving meeting. It's a difficult meeting to schedule because often there are many teachers who work with each struggling reader. There should be two or three staff members who attend all the meetings; my recommendation is that the principal and RTI coordinator be present at all meetings. The principal is ultimately in charge of allocating resources and has to be present to make these decisions. The RTI coordinator needs to be present to keep track of the decisions and any implications on groupings that may result from the meeting. If the RTI coordinator isn't the reading expert in your building, then a reading specialist may also need to be present. The teachers who work with a student may include the classroom teacher, an intervention teacher, and an ESL or special education teacher, if the student is receiving those services. Sometimes a school psychologist or speech-language pathologist is also present.

It's important that the classroom teacher be present even if he is not the one providing intervention instruction to the student. One of our consultants shared a story that happened while conducting a walk-through to observe intervention groups. The reading coach had specifically asked her to take a look at a kindergarten student who had been stuck in a very low phonological awareness group for approximately six weeks. They couldn't figure out why he couldn't pass the skill level. Our consultant watched the student work with the interventionist and observed that any time he was given the word *my*, he combined it with the word that followed. They puzzled over why the student must not realize that *my* is an individual word. Later in the day, while discussing the example at the kindergarten grade-level team meeting, the student's classroom teacher said, "Of course . . . his sister's name is Miangel, and it's one word!" As the consultant reported, "The greatest thing was that it provided a *perfect* opportunity for me to discuss how important teacher involvement is in intervention instruction!"

Scheduling the Meeting

Most schools designate a time during the school day when problem-solving meetings occur. For example, it may be that time is allocated for these meetings to occur every two weeks on Thursday mornings between nine o'clock and eleven o'clock. If each meeting is scheduled for 20 minutes, then the team will be able to consider six students during this allocated time every two weeks. Any teacher with concerns about a student can sign up for a time slot on the schedule. The RTI coordinator will arrange to have one intervention teacher combine two groups for that morning in order to free up a teacher to go from room to room to release different teachers to attend the meetings. If the schedule is e-mailed to all staff the day before the meetings, then everyone will know what they need to do so that these meetings can occur. Some schools schedule these meetings on early release days or arrange them based on collaboration or planning time.

Meeting Expectations

Teachers need to know what to bring to the meeting and what to expect. It's important for teachers to prepare their data before they walk into the meeting room. That means that data reports, intervention logs, and bulleted talking points are ready to go, so the meeting runs efficiently. Some schools use a process of e-mailing the data in advance of the meeting.

It's important for teachers to prepare their data before they walk into the meeting room.

During the meeting, four main topics should be covered. The agenda should include the following:

1. Recap of the progress-monitoring data for the student
2. Overview of interventions provided to date
3. Discussion of what more can be provided to intensify intervention
4. Decision

The first three topics can be covered in about five minutes each. In the final few minutes, the group reaches a decision and then staff rotates for the next meeting. So that sound decisions can be made, I'll explain in more detail what is needed for each of the first three agenda topics.

Reports for Data Recap on a Student

Start the problem-solving meeting with progress-monitoring graphs (Figure 6.2) showing the student's rate of progress and why, with this current rate of improvement, the gap won't close and benchmark will not be reached. The following information should be shown on the progress-monitoring graph:

- Student's score at the starting point of intervention (first bold black dot near the bottom left of the graph)
- Goal, or the score the student needs to attain to reach proficiency (large bull's eye near the top right of the graph in the gray-shaded band, which represents the benchmark)
- Data points for each progress-monitoring assessment date (bold black dots)
- Aim line drawn from the student's initial score to the goal of proficient score (bold black line connecting the student's starting score with the goal)
- Trend line of the student's actual progress-monitoring data points (dotted line connecting the data points)

Start the problem-solving meeting with progress-monitoring graphs showing the student's rate of progress and why, with this current rate of improvement, the gap won't close and benchmark will not be reached.

Figure 6.2 Sample Student Progress-Monitoring Graph

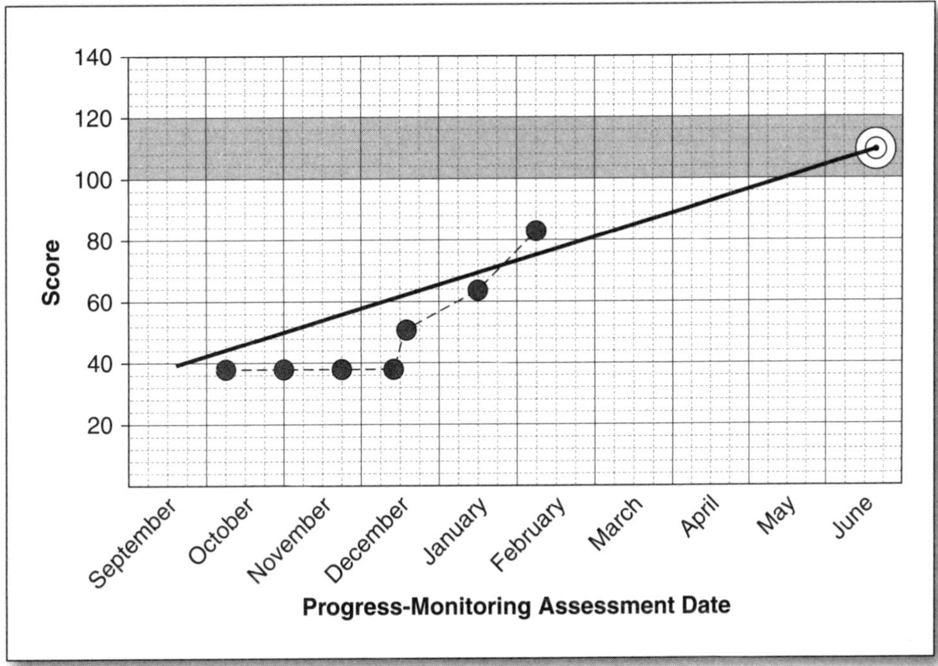

There are two lines:

- The aim line (sometimes called the goal line) is the necessary rate of progress.
- The trend line is the student's actual rate of progress.

When the slope of the trend line is substantially below the needed aim line, the student will not close the gap and catch up to grade level. With the current rate of progress, the student will not reach benchmark by the end of the year; the value is in realizing this early enough in the year to make changes that will help the student shift to a path of greater progress.

The progress-monitoring graph should be prepared based on the indicator that is most relevant, which will vary depending on grade level and time of year. Monitor whatever skill is the focus of the intervention group. For example, if a third-grade student has been placed in a vowel-team group, then the progress-monitoring graph includes data from the phonics diagnostic screener for vowel teams. It's helpful if, every once in a while, the main skill (such as ORF) is also given to see how far below grade level the student's reading is.

If you need to calculate a weekly goal, take the difference in the beginning score and the goal score and divide by the number of weeks remaining. For example, a third-grade student who is in a fluency group has an initial score of 70 words correct per minute (wcpm) with a benchmark at year-end of 110 wcpm. The difference of 40 words (110 − 70) is divided by 16 (because there are 16 weeks left in the school year). The goal is to improve 2.5 words per week to make benchmark, or proficiency, level. If after 3 weeks, the student has made no progress, the teacher should be concerned because now only 13 weeks remain and, in order to reach 110 wcpm by the end of the school year, the student's required weekly progress rate has increased from 2.5 to 3 words a week.

One of the most powerful graphs a teacher can show is the accelerated rate of progress of the other members of the struggling student's group. Most of the time, all the students placed in a particular small group together started in that group with about the same score on a diagnostic screener. Assuming the struggling student didn't have an attendance issue, all the students received the same instruction. The other students made progress and were exited, but this one student had to continue for another round—this is powerful evidence that this student may be experiencing a learning issue. If even more rounds of intervention were required, the data begins to converge, showing that this student's skills are not responding to the intensity of the current Tier II group. This data makes the case that the struggling student needs more intense intervention, and if intensifying Tier II instruction doesn't bring results, then the student needs to be moved to Tier III. Eventually, if this pattern repeats several times even in Tier III, the data begins to point to the possibility of a learning disability.

One of the most powerful graphs a teacher can show is the accelerated rate of progress of the other members of the struggling student's group.

Which Interventions Have Been Provided to Date?

An important part of the problem-solving meeting is for one of the participants to be able to provide a summary of the interventions the student has received to date. The information that the team needs includes the student's initial skill-group placement, the number of students in that group, the materials used for instruction, and the intervention teacher. A chart that shows how long she stayed in that initial group, and then the same information about each successive group she's been in, is needed.

Tracking this amount of information may seem cumbersome to teachers. To avoid overwhelming teachers or overlooking information, it's important to adopt some form of record keeping from the outset. We recommend using intervention logs that include all of the aforementioned information in a manner that takes very little time and that can be filled out during the intervention group time. The intervention log should include the following information:

- Student name and attendance
- Focus of the group

- Number of students in the group and names of all the group members
- Number of minutes intervention was provided
- Bulleted list of observation notes

Figure 6.3 provides an example of an intervention log. This is a three-week log that is contained on one sheet of paper for the entire group for a three-week period. It's important to keep the intervention logs up to date at all times because it's an even greater burden to try to recreate the information later. The problem is that you never know at the outset which students will not make progress and for whom you'll need these records.

How Can We Intensify Intervention Instruction?

When a student's rate of progress isn't sufficient, the first question to ask is whether instruction can be intensified within the same group.

Figure 6.3 Sample Three-Week Intervention Log

95% GROUP INC.

Interventionist:

Group Focus	Focus:	Focus:	Focus:
Lesson Plan and/or Materials			
Dates for the Week	Dates: Nov 1-5, 06	Dates:	Dates:
Record minutes of intervention for each day	Mon. 30 / Tue. 25 / Wed. / Thur. / Fri.	Mon. / Tue. / Wed. / Thur. / Fri.	Mon. / Tue. / Wed. / Thur. / Fri.
PSI™ or PASI™ Skill Number and Score Student Name: Betsy BM / PM / PM / PM 19 / Seg / 5 /	(M) (T) W Th F Repeats words when she stumbles.	M T W Th F	M T W Th F
Student Name: Faith BM / PM / PM / PM 16 / Seg / 8 /	(M) (T) W Th F Faith is not missing any words; needs to work on fluency.	M T W Th F	M T W Th F
Student Name: Carol BM / PM / PM / PM 29 / Seg / 5 /	(M) T W Th F Carol has missed 6 days of school in the past 2 weeks.	M T W Th F	M T W Th F
Student Name: Alan BM / PM / PM / PM 19 / Seg / 6 /	(M) (T) W Th F	M T W Th F	M T W Th F
Student Name: BM / PM / PM / PM	M T W Th F	M T W Th F	M T W Th F
Student Name: BM / PM / PM / PM	M T W Th F	M T W Th F	M T W Th F

Source: 95 Percent Group Inc., 2005–2010. Reprinted with permission.

There are several ways to intensify instruction, including adding time, reducing the group size, changing the instructor, or changing materials or programs. Generally, the first one to try is to add time. A student can attend two intervention time slots instead of one, sometimes called "double dipping." If the team decides to try a second intervention slot for a few weeks, then the teacher will need to monitor the student's progress closely to see whether adding time is helping. At times, a team may decide to increase the frequency of progress monitoring because more data points make it easier to get a more accurate trend line, especially when a student's scores fluctuate widely.

There are several ways to intensify instruction, including adding time, reducing the group size, changing the instructor, or changing materials or programs.

Getting Started With Problem-Solving Meetings

The 15-minute agenda described earlier is tight and efficient. Many principals ask how to streamline these meetings and help teachers learn how to make the most of the 15 minutes they have to talk about a student. Have you ever been in a meeting when a teacher talks on and on about a student's troubling home life and recounts conversations rather than sticking to the facts of the data? This is a challenge, yet training teachers to focus on the desired content of these meetings can be viewed as a process that teachers need to be taught through explicit instruction and modeling. Decide how you want your meetings to progress, and meet with each grade level to tell them. Present the agenda format and a sample packet of information that you want them to bring, including the progress-monitoring graphs and intervention logs. Consider videotaping an effective meeting and having the grade-level team leader show the video at a meeting. Then once you begin the meetings, adhere to the schedule. Don't go over the time limit for any reason, because if you do, you'll be rewarding the exact behavior you want to avoid. These meetings work only if there are advance preparations and efficient teacher presentations.

RTI TEAM MEETINGS

Each school's RTI team will have periodic meetings, probably monthly, to talk about the implementation. The purpose of these meetings is to focus on whether, overall, the school is on track in implementing RTI and to examine whether each grade level has all the procedures in place so that implementation runs smoothly. RTI team members look at student progress of the grade level as a whole, as well as the effectiveness of their procedures. It's not unusual for one grade level to adjust easily and implement smoothly while another one struggles. If there is friction among the teachers on a team, the RTI process will be more difficult than on teams that collaborate well.

Another function of the RTI team meeting is to coordinate between the grade levels. If the kindergarten team's student data is not where it needs to be, it will impact the first-grade team as students start the next year with deficits. In many schools, we used to hear about the second-grade slump; we've observed that often the second-grade slump is really a first-grade hangover. If students leave first grade behind where they should be, their ability to make sufficient progress in second grade will be impaired. For each grade level progressively, catching students up becomes harder and harder. Not only does the gap continue to widen, but teachers find it difficult to have enough groups to address all the possible gaps. Therefore, the RTI team must address issues of a single grade-level's implementation because those issues spill over to the next grade level.

Some decisions should be made schoolwide. Therefore, staff members must have a common understanding about which skills must be mastered at a given grade level. We recommend that the following skills should be mastered at each grade level:

- *Kindergarten:* Students in kindergarten need to master the entire phonological awareness continuum through phoneme substitution, letter-naming fluency, a minimum of 25 to 50 high-frequency sight words, and print awareness.
- *Grade 1:* Students in first grade need to be able to decode in a blended manner words with short vowels including CVC, consonant blends and consonant digraphs, and the long vowel silent-*e* pattern; read at least 125 high-frequency sight words; and demonstrate comprehension of sequence and main idea.
- *Grade 2:* Students in second grade should be able to decode all one-syllable word patterns, develop increasing fluency in text, continue to expand their high-frequency sight word recognition, and broaden their comprehension skills.
- *Grade 3:* Students in third grade should be able to read multisyllable words, continue to improve their fluency, and deepen their comprehension skills.

Staff members must have a common understanding about which skills must be mastered at a given grade level.

It's critical that everyone uses the same assessments so that each grade can send meaningful records to the receiving teachers. This will prevent loss of time at the beginning of the year in identifying the needs of students who've already been in intervention groups.

CONCLUSION

Discussing data should be part of the culture of grade-level team meetings. The popularity of professional learning communities comes just in time for RTI; PLCs are a framework for moving the dialogue from "administrivia" to student learning, and RTI can be the content of the dialogue. At grade-level team meetings, the teachers should regularly talk about the progress of the whole grade level of students. When one student's rate of progress is insufficient, the teacher should bring that student's data to a brainstorming session during the problem-solving meeting. This chapter included ideas about agenda topics and tips on how to teach school staff members to prepare for these short, efficient conversations about students.

Additional materials and resources related to *Jumpstart RTI: Using RTI in Your Elementary School Right Now* can be found at http://my.95percentgroup.com/Jumpstart.

7

Referring a Student for Special Education Testing

Chapter 6 discussed the use of data in grade-level team meetings, where the progress of the students at an entire grade level is examined, and also in problem-solving meetings, where the focus is on one individual student. The topic covered in this chapter is how the RTI framework supports the identification and qualification of students with learning disabilities who may need special education services (see Figure 7.1).

RTI AND SPECIAL EDUCATION

It's possible to claim that the roots of RTI lie in special education. But that's not the whole picture. Although the reauthorization of the Individuals with Disabilities Education Act (IDEA, 2004) certainly paved the way for RTI, the practice of teaching small groups based on identifying a student's needs identified using assessment data is not a new idea. What IDEA 2004 did was to provide an incentive, or even a mandate, for state governments to require districts to adopt an RTI framework for delivering general education instruction in tiers and using progress-monitoring data to identify students who may need special education.

The relationship between RTI and special education clearly merges in problem-solving meetings, which are linked to the process of referring a

Figure 7.1 Facilitation and Referrals

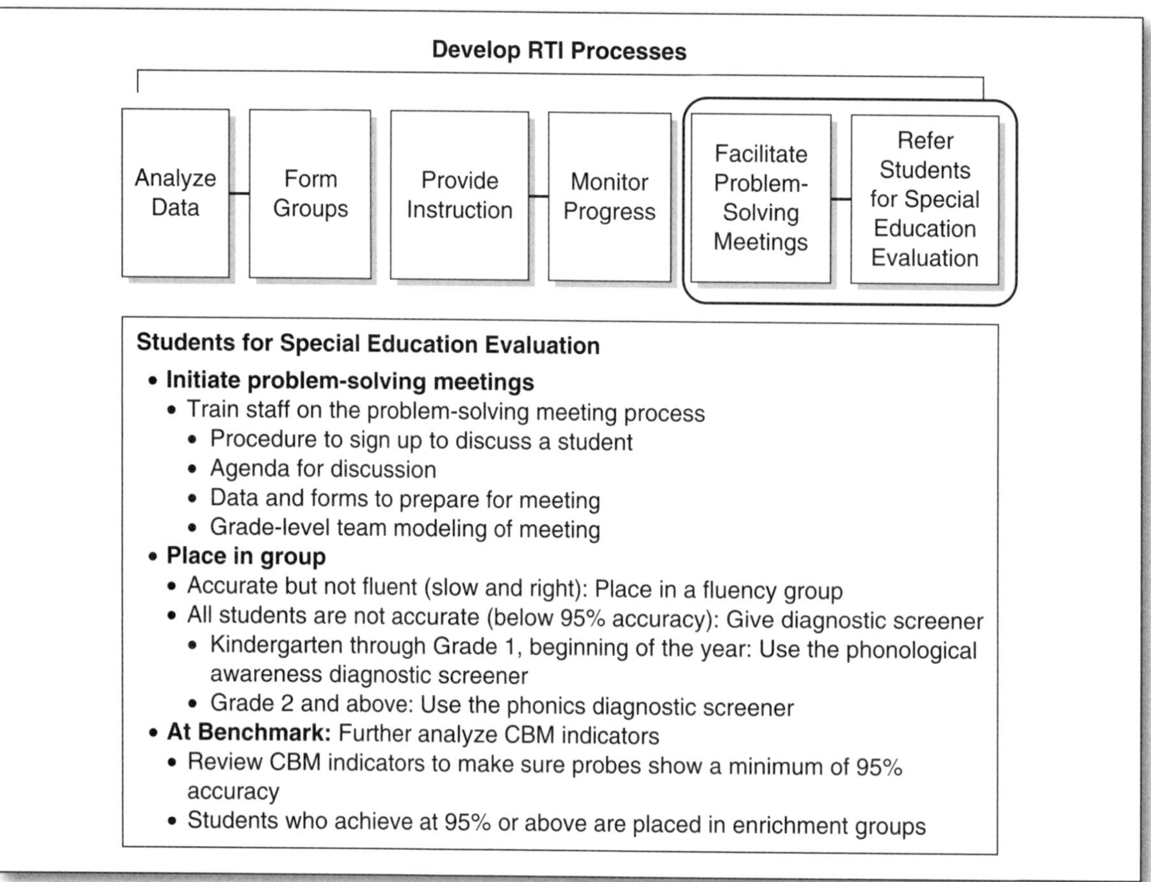

Students for Special Education Evaluation

- **Initiate problem-solving meetings**
  - Train staff on the problem-solving meeting process
    - Procedure to sign up to discuss a student
    - Agenda for discussion
    - Data and forms to prepare for meeting
    - Grade-level team modeling of meeting
- **Place in group**
  - Accurate but not fluent (slow and right): Place in a fluency group
  - All students are not accurate (below 95% accuracy): Give diagnostic screener
    - Kindergarten through Grade 1, beginning of the year: Use the phonological awareness diagnostic screener
    - Grade 2 and above: Use the phonics diagnostic screener
- **At Benchmark:** Further analyze CBM indicators
  - Review CBM indicators to make sure probes show a minimum of 95% accuracy
  - Students who achieve at 95% or above are placed in enrichment groups

student to child study for possible qualification for special education services. With the reauthorization of IDEA 2004, states can no longer require districts to use the IQ-achievement discrepancy formula to qualify students for special education services. While the discrepancy formula cannot be required, its use is also not prohibited. However, IDEA 2004 encourages the use of an RTI framework.

IDEA 2004 also includes language about the importance of intervention instruction that is preventive, or that could prevent some students from ending up on individualized education plans (IEPs) and receiving special education services. Up to 15% of the special education budget can be spent on prevention, which means that up to 15% of special education staff time can be dedicated to *delivering intervention to students* not on IEPs. The prevention budget can also be used to fund professional development on RTI for general and special education staff or to purchase materials used for intervention instruction to help prevent learning disabilities.

IDEA 2004 requires that appropriate instruction be provided before a student can be considered learning disabled. Lack of appropriate instruction must be eliminated as a possible cause of low achievement. When a student's skills fail to respond to intervention instruction, this important evidence points to a possible learning disability. The multitier approach of moving students from Tier II to Tier III is a framework for providing more intense intervention to determine whether a student can master the skills with increasing levels of support. This is why documentation of the small-group instruction a student receives in a general education setting is critical. Progress-monitoring data that shows a low rate of progress with increasingly intense instruction doesn't by itself demonstrate that there is a learning disability. It supports a case to consider a learning disability. In other words, it presents a compelling case for why a student should be tested.

Lack of appropriate instruction must be eliminated as a possible cause of low achievement.

Each state approaches RTI differently. Most states encourage districts to implement RTI by requiring them to submit plans that specify timetables for when they need to have processes in place. A couple of states eliminated the use of the IQ-achievement discrepancy formula (Colorado and West Virginia). Many states leave it to the districts to decide the type of educational testing that should be done. Therefore, some districts continue to use IQ testing to a greater extent than other districts. Regardless of whether IQ tests are given, there still needs to be an appropriate battery of tests to confirm a learning disability that is suspected, but not confirmed, by the low rate of progress and evidence of difficulty in learning.

Regardless of whether IQ tests are given, there still needs to be an appropriate battery of tests to confirm a learning disability that is suspected, but not confirmed, by the low rate of progress and evidence of difficulty in learning.

Because the data collected in the general education setting that documents a lack of response to interventions is critical, we recommend that districts establish a standard intervention log and progress-monitoring graphs (see Chapter 6). It's impossible to know at the outset which students will later be referred. It's very difficult, if not impossible, for teachers to create the logs documenting the information after the fact. Having an efficient intervention log that is used for all students receiving intervention instruction is critical.

Having an efficient intervention log that is used for all students receiving intervention instruction is critical.

School psychologists have commented on how much teacher's dialogue at child study meetings has changed after RTI is in place. There is less anecdotal information, and teachers are more confident that a student shows signs of a learning disability because of the data. Table 7.1 provides a list of helpful information that teachers can bring to child study meetings.

Table 7.1 List of Helpful Information for Child Study Meetings

Information	Description
Progress-monitoring data	• Progress-monitoring graphs showing that a student's actual rate of progress was almost flat, or substantially lower than the rate required by the aim line • Graphs showing that the student's progress was seriously lower than all the other students who started in the same group
Intervention instruction	• Charts showing the number of rounds a student stayed in a group for the same skill
Intervention logs	• Size of group for each week • Number of minutes of instruction received weekly based on student's attendance • Changes in intensity by reduced group size, increased time, or use of different materials
Problem-solving meeting information	• Decisions about moving a student from Tier II to Tier III • Discussion notes

When all of this data is available in a standard format as outlined in Table 7.1, the child study team's meeting is efficient, and they can effectively determine whether a student should be referred for testing for a possible learning disability.

Decrease in Referrals for Testing

One of the most important benefits of RTI is that the number of students referred for testing and those qualifying for special education should drop when small-group intervention is provided in the general education setting. One of our clients has shared data about this exact outcome. We began working with an intermediate unit (IU) in Michigan four years ago (*intermediate unit* is the name given to organizations that are regional service centers funded by the state government to offer professional development and sometimes special education cooperative services). The special education department of this IU invited us to provide some overview training to participants from the 10 districts that it serves.

After some initial overview workshops defining RTI, exploring the multitier delivery model, and discussing data-analysis procedures, we began to talk about how the IU could further support the implementation of RTI in its districts. The IU decided to offer an opportunity for one pilot school in each district to receive additional professional development to initiate RTI in kindergarten and first grade. An application process was used to identify the districts that were ready to make the commitment; the districts then proposed the school that would be the pilot school in the application. The goal was that by supporting full implementation in one pilot school in each district, the other schools could implement on their own. Out of 10 districts, 7 decided to participate with one pilot school in the first cohort group.

The pilot sites received an all-day workshop for kindergarten and first-grade teachers, quarterly administrator training, and on-site follow-up three times a year to coach and mentor classroom teachers. Our company provided all the professional development under the coordination of the IU. The project has continued in order to support the scaling up to Grades 2 and 3 at these original sites plus the addition of two more cohort groups to bring on new schools each year. The IU staff tracked the effectiveness of the implementation by collecting a variety of data, including increases in students' *DIBELS* scores, as well as special education referrals and qualifications. Table 7.2 shows that by the third year, the number of students referred for testing for a possible learning disability was approximately one-third the number in the initial year (27 versus 73). In addition, the accuracy of the referrals has increased (from 46% to 52%).

By the third year, the number of students referred for testing for a possible learning disability was approximately one-third the number in the initial year (27 versus 73).

The student data also showed a significant increase in students reaching benchmark in all grade levels of implementation. All schools reported that grade-level teams collaborated more during this process than before. Three of the seven districts began implementing RTI districtwide by the end of the second year, and nearly all the remaining districts have expanded after the third year. It is clear that students improved across a wide variety of indicators.

CHANGE IN ROLE OF SPECIAL EDUCATION STAFF

The role of special education staff in the implementation of RTI varies widely across districts. RTI is led by the special education district directors in less than 10% of the clients we serve. These individuals tend to be

Table 7.2 Special Education Referral Rate in Michigan Cohort Group I

Cohort I (Seven Schools)	2006–2007	2007–2008	2008–2009
Number of students referred	73	71	27
Number of students qualified	34	26	14
Percentage qualified of those referred	46	37	52

unusual visionaries of what's right and what's wrong about the current special education system in the United States. In the vast majority of districts, the curriculum department at the district office spearheads the implementation. While it's important that RTI is not seen as just another special education initiative, it's equally important that it should be a cooperative effort of both general and special education. RTI, clearly, cannot be done effectively without leadership from general education, because the majority of the assessment and instruction activities happen in the general education setting. However, because of the impact on the referral process, special education must be a key player as well.

RTI, clearly, cannot be done effectively without leadership from general education, because the majority of the assessment and instruction activities happen in the general education setting.

The future role of special education teachers may change because of RTI, but the degree of change is not yet clear. Special education teachers may serve as members of assessment teams and be involved in universal screening and diagnostic assessments. They may provide intervention instruction by working with some of the small groups during the intervention-block times, meaning that they'd be working with some students not on IEPs. They may teach Tier III groups. Currently, special education teachers in some schools serve as resources or sounding boards for teachers who seek help with certain struggling students.

Unfortunately, when RTI first emerged, the lack of clarity about how this process would interact with special education left a great deal of uncertainty. The following concerns and fears expressed by special education teachers need to be addressed:

- Work load issues of covering current IEP case load plus expectation to teach more students
- Dilution of focus on the students who need them the most
- Concern about the increased role of general education teachers in the referral and qualification process
- Loss of job in the future resulting from fewer students on IEPs

During the past 5 to 10 years, much research has shown that students in special education do not catch up and that the gains nationwide have been minimal despite the major investment of funds. These are large-scale studies, and clearly, there are many examples in individual schools and districts where students on IEPs are making excellent progress. Many times, special education teachers haven't been provided the training in reading instruction that they need to do their jobs, and reading difficulties are the greatest area of need for students on IEPs for learning disabilities. Too few schools and districts have invested in training special education teachers in multisensory structured language approaches based on Orton-Gillingham techniques.

In some cases, the instruction in Tier II and III is more targeted and focused than what a special education teacher is able to provide in a traditional resource-room setting, where there are eight or more students whose needs vary widely. We recommend that, when possible, students on IEPs should be placed in an RTI group to receive targeted small-group instruction in their area of greatest need according to diagnostic data. One reading coach reported that a parent of a student on an IEP requested to have her child get the Tier II targeted small-group instruction and give up the IEP minutes, if there weren't enough minutes in the day to have both.

We recommend that, when possible, students on IEPs should be placed in an RTI group to receive targeted small-group instruction in their area of greatest need according to diagnostic data.

Many special education teachers embrace RTI because they know that it is right for students. Many have had the experience of working with a student on an IEP who may not have a serious learning disability, and if only the right kind of small-group intervention had been provided at the right time, this student might not have ended up in the special education system at all.

COMMUNICATION WITH PARENTS

Schools have many questions about communicating with parents about RTI groups because they are not sure whether to make their approach parallel to the approach that special education uses. Although communicating with parents about a student's participation in a Tier II or III group is important, there are some clear differences between RTI and special education. Our suggestions are listed in Table 7.3.

By including an overview of RTI in the parent handbook, the administration can refer parents to this document when explaining that the assessment and small-group instruction are part of the normal practices of the school. This description can be short, but it should mention that the school uses universal and diagnostic screeners and that, based on the screening data, students are placed in small groups for differentiated instruction. If the school uses the walk-to-intervention model, it's easy to explain that *all* students are in small groups—even the students who score above benchmark.

Don't ask parents to sign a permission form for assessment or small-group placement. If the parent says no, the school's hands are tied, and you'll have to deny the very help that the student needs to avert a larger problem later. Since assessment and instruction happen during the school day, they don't require permission. A parallel example

Table 7.3 Recommended Communication Plan With Parents

Event	Communication With Parents
General information to parents	• Include description of RTI in parent handbook • Briefly mention and describe assessment and small-group differentiated instruction at parent curriculum open houses
Universal and diagnostic screening	• No permission form needed
Placement of student in Tier II or Tier III group	• No permission form needed • Parent notified upon first placement into an intervention group
Movement of student from Tier II to Tier III group	• No permission form needed • Parent notified of change in placement to more intense group because of lower rate of progress than desirable
Parent conferences	• Show progress-monitoring graph to parents during regularly scheduled parent-teacher conferences
Referral of student to child study team for consideration of testing for special education	• Permission form required, according to special education protocols • Follow all protocols established by special education process

is that students are given state assessments without permission forms, and students are placed in small groups during core instruction time without permission forms. We recommend informing parents about placement into an intervention group because they may hear about it from the student, who may casually say something about going to a different teacher during the day. Notification and permission are two different things.

Teachers report that parents appreciate seeing progress-monitoring graphs for students who are receiving intervention. Even if the parent doesn't understand what phoneme segmentation is, it's easy for them to relate to a graph that shows their child's starting point, the aim line, the ending goal, and the rate of progress as reflected in the slope of the line joining the progress-monitoring points. Principals have reported very successful meetings with parents who expressed concerns. Hearing and seeing the assessment data that is collected to pinpoint skill deficits and learning about the focused instruction that is being provided to their child to address deficits allays parents' concerns. Most parents appreciate the concreteness of this data. One principal reported that he talked about the medical-model analogy with a parent. He explained that this is like well-baby checkups; we are making sure that the child meets all the interim milestones in reading so that he doesn't move to a later grade with gaps.

CONCLUSION

Although the legal foundation for RTI is rooted in IDEA 2004, a special education federal legislation, RTI must be a coordinated effort of general and special education staff. During the next few years, school staff will need to remain flexible as we determine the assessments that will be completed to diagnose a learning disability and the way in which special educators' jobs will be affected. Most of the activities are conducted within the general education setting, yet what happens there must be documented in a way that assures that the data filters into the referral process for making decisions about which students should be tested. Communication with parents should follow a mode of providing information rather than asking permission up until the student is referred for testing for a learning disability. At that point, all the normal procedures for parent permission will begin.

Additional materials and resources related to *Jumpstart RTI: Using RTI in Your Elementary School Right Now* can be found at http://my.95percentgroup.com/Jumpstart.

Bibliography

American Recovery and Reinvestment Act of 2009. Pub. L. 111–5, 26 USC (2009).

Batsche, G., Elliott, J., Graden, J. L., Grimes, J., Kovaleski, J. F., Prasse, D., et al. (2006). *Response to intervention: Policy considerations and implementation.* Alexandria, VA: National Association of State Directors of Special Education.

Beck, I., McKeown, M., & Kucan, L. (2002). *Bringing words to life: Robust vocabulary instruction.* New York: Guilford Press.

Bentum, K. E., & Aaron, P. G. (2003). Does reading instruction in learning disability resource rooms really work? A longitudinal study. *Reading Psychology, 24*(3–4), 361–382.

Cushman, K. (2010, February). The strive of it: What conditions inspire teens to practice toward perfection? *Educational Leadership, 67*(5), 50–55. Retrieved from http://www.ascd.org/publications/educational_leadership/feb10/vol67/num05/%C2%A3The_Strive_of_It%C2%A3.aspx

Developmental Reading Assessment (2nd ed.). (2005). Saddle River, NJ: Pearson Education. Available from www.pearsonschool.com

Erwin, T. (2007, August 6). The five WHYS and HOWS for principals [PowerPoint]. In S. Hall & T. Erwin, *Reading First: Districtwide! How?* presentation at Just Read, Florida conference at Shoal Creek Conference Center, Orlando, FL.

Francis, D. J., Fletcher, J. M., Stuebing, K. K., Lyon, G. R., Shaywitz, B. A., & Shaywitz, S. E. (2005). Psychometric approaches to the identification of LD: IQ and achievement scores are not sufficient. *Journal of Learning Disabilities, 38*(2), 98–108.

Gersten, R., & Dimino, J. A. (2006). RTI (response to intervention): Rethinking special education for students with reading difficulties (again). *Reading Research Quarterly, 41*(1), 99–108.

Good, R., H., & Kaminski, R. A. (2002a). *DIBELS oral reading fluency passages for first through third grades.* Technical Report 10. Eugene: University of Oregon.

Good, R. H., & Kaminski, R. A. (Eds.). (2002b). *Dynamic indicators of basic early literacy skills* (6th ed.). Eugene, OR: Institute for the Development of Educational Achievement. Available from http://dibels.uoregon.edu

Graves, M. (2006). *The vocabulary book: Learning and instruction.* New York: Teachers College Press.

Hall, S. (2006). *I've DIBEL'd, now what?* Longmont, CO: Sopris West, Cambium Learning.

Hall, S. (2008). *Implementing response to intervention: A principal's guide.* Thousand Oaks, CA: Corwin.

Individuals with Disabilities Education Act of 2004, 20 U.S.C § 1400 et. seq.

Kavale, K. (1990). Effectiveness of special education. In T. B. Gutkin & C. R. Reynolds (Eds.), *Handbook of school psychology* (2nd ed.; pp. 868–898). New York: Wiley.

Lyon, G. R., Fletcher, J. M., Shaywitz, B., Shaywitz, S., Torgesen, J., Wood, F., et al. (2001). Rethinking learning disabilities. In C. E. Finn Jr., A. J. Rotherham & C. R. Hokanson Jr., *Rethinking special education for a new century* (pp. 259–280). Washington, DC: Thomas B. Fordham Foundation/ Progressive Policy Institute.

Mesmer, E. M., & Mesmer, H. A. (2008–2009). Response to intervention (RTI): What teachers of reading need to know. *The Reading Teacher, 62*(4), 280–290.

National Institute for Literacy. (2009). *Developing early literacy: Report of the Early Literacy Panel.* Washington, DC: Author.

95 Percent Group Inc. (2005a). *95 Percent Group's basic phonological awareness continuum.* Lincolnshire, IL: Author.

95 Percent Group Inc. (2005b). *95 Percent Group's phonics continuum.* Lincolnshire, IL: Author.

95 Percent Group Inc. (2007a). *Grouping form.* Lincolnshire, IL: Author.

95 Percent Group Inc. (2007b). *Phonics screener for intervention.* Lincolnshire, IL: Author.

95 Percent Group Inc. (2007c). *Phonological awareness screener for intervention.* Lincolnshire, IL: Author.

95 Percent Group Inc. (2007d). *Sample school master schedule.* Lincolnshire, IL: Author.

95 Percent Group Inc. (2008). *Blueprint for intervention: Routine cards and guide.* Lincolnshire, IL: Author.

95 Percent Group Inc. (2009). *Blueprint for intervention: Phonological awareness.* Lincolnshire, IL: Author.

No Child Left Behind Act of 2001. 20 U.S.C. § 6301 et seq. (2002).

Stanovich, K. (2005). The future of a mistake: Will discrepancy measurement continue to make the learning disabilities field a pseudoscience? *Learning Disability Quarterly, 28*(2), 103–106.

University of Oregon Center on Teaching and Learning. (2002). *Dynamic indicators of basic early literacy skills data system* (6th ed.). Eugene, OR: Author. Available from https://dibels.uoregon.edu

Vaughn, S., & Guchs, L. S. (2003). Redefining learning disabilities as inadequate response to instruction: The promise and potential problems. *Learning Disabilities Research and Practice, 18*(3), 137–146.

Vellutino, F. R., Scanlong, D. M., & Lyon, G. R. (2000). Differentiating between difficult-to-remediate and readily remediated poor readers: More evidence against the IQ-discrepancy definition of reading disability. *Journal of Learning Disabilities, 33*(3), 223–238.

Willingham, D. (2006/2007, Winter). The usefulness of brief instruction in reading comprehension strategies. *American Educator, 30*(4).

Index

Note: Page numbers followed by an *f* indicate figures, and those followed by a *t* refer to tables.

The Corwin logo—a raven striding across an open book—represents the union of courage and learning. Corwin is committed to improving education for all learners by publishing books and other professional development resources for those serving the field of PreK–12 education. By providing practical, hands-on materials, Corwin continues to carry out the promise of its motto: **"Helping Educators Do Their Work Better."**